THE

CREED OF THE CHRISTIAN

BY

CHARLES GORE, D.D.
LORD BISHOP OF BIRMINGHAM

WIPF & STOCK · Eugene, Oregon

Wipf and Stock Publishers
199 W 8th Ave, Suite 3
Eugene, OR 97401

The Creed of the Christian
By Gore, Charles
ISBN 13: 978-1-61097-443-1
Publication date 4/20/2011
Previously published by Wells Gardner, Dalton & Co., 1905

PREFACE

THIS book consists of articles entitled ' Fundamentals,'
published in *Goodwill* in 1894-95. I have assented to their
republication, and have revised them and made some
additions to them for that purpose, simply because they
appear to have been found useful by Christians of different
kinds anxious for fuller information about the meaning of
their religion.

C. G.

St. Cecilia's Day, 1895.

CONTENTS

THE

CREED OF THE CHRISTIAN

WHAT ARE DOGMAS?

'Tho' truths in manhood darkly join,
    Deep-seated in our mystic frame,
    We yield all blessing to the name
Of Him that made them current coin:

For Wisdom dealt with mortal powers,
    Where truth in closest words shall fail,
    When truth embodied in a tale
Shall enter in at lowly doors.'

THERE was once a wise man called Socrates. He was
an Athenian, and the people of Athens were intellectual
and philosophical to a degree never yet equalled among
men. Naturally, therefore, they were fond of argument,
and held the power of brilliant and persuasive speech in
the highest esteem.

But intellectual and brilliant as they were, they were
not in the habit of thinking or speaking *exactly*. They did
not know what they did know and what they did not.
They mistook a well-sounding argument for a real truth.
This Socrates saw, and he felt it to be his mission to
convince his fellow-citizens of ignorance, to teach them
to define their thoughts and to use words exactly. If they
could get into the habit of exact thought, he saw they
would be able to distinguish between a merely plausible
argument and the truth, and would begin to make real
progress in knowledge. So he would always question men
about the words they used. He would stop the flow of

5

some eloquent speech about courage with the question, 'What is courage?' And very soon it appeared, under his cross-questioning, that the eloquent speaker had very vague ideas what courage really means. If he merely cared for his reputation, he grew very cross at being thus shown up; but if he was a man sincerely anxious to get at the truth, it made him serious and careful, and he began to make progress.

Now, we need a nineteenth-century Socrates. We are, many of us, keenly interested in intellectual questions, in politics, social matters, or religion. We are captivated by a ready speaker with his flow of words. We catch up ideas, and repeat them. But we do not think exactly; we do not use words exactly; so we do not see through fallacies; we do not distinguish true arguments from sophistries.

I will take an example. We often, in religious discussions, hear or read of denunciations of dogmas: 'barren dogmas!' 'mere dogmas!' 'ecclesiastical dogmas!' 'incomprehensible dogmas!' 'irrational dogmas!' 'dogmas that a plain man can't see the use of!' Now, in this sort of language there is great confusion of thought, and therefore it leads to no real progress. A Socrates who should cross-examine one of us would convince him that the evil was not the 'dogma' itself, but the misuse of it. Every good thing can be misused—even liberty. So can dogma. But it is a good thing misused, none the less.

A dogma is a (supposed) truth stated in such a plain way that it can be used as a tenet, or part of the creed of a society of men, and be taken for granted in all the affairs of life, and serve as a common standard of reference. Thus, the statement which forms the basis of the American Declaration of Independence, and so of the Constitution of the United States—the statement that 'All men are born free and equal'—is a dogma. It is a statement of a (supposed) truth turned into the tenet of a society of men. It has become a social creed. No society of men can get on without ideas that are in this way taken for granted. Thus, it is evident that what is evil is not dogma, but some misuse of dogma.

A religious dogma, for example, may be (1) untrue, or ill-grounded and unwarranted; or (2) it may be useless and inapplicable to human life; or (3) it may be uttered by a teacher in such a way as not to commend it to the conscience and reason of his hearers.

If it is untrue or uncertain, it ought not to be uttered as a tenet of the Christian society; if it is really inapplicable to human life, it is certainly not a tenet of that most practical of all societies—the Christian Church; if it is uttered offensively, the teacher needs to be taught how to 'commend himself to every man's conscience.' But all this misuse of dogma does not come near to touching its real value rightly used.

In fact, nothing is so necessary for human society as the common recognition of truths, converted into maxims or accepted principles to inspire and regulate the common life.

Darius the king is said to have summoned all his great men from out his vast empire to decide which of three young men gave the best answer to the question, 'What is the strongest thing in the world?' The first wrote, 'Wine is the strongest.' The second wrote, 'The king is strongest.' The third wrote, 'Women are strongest: but above all things Truth beareth away the victory.'

Each in turn tried to prove his case. But the last proposition finally commended itself to the judgment of the assembled host. 'And all the people then shouted, and said, "Great is the Truth, and doth prevail." '*

This is a right decision. In our days we do not need to be convinced that wine—or, at any rate, beer and spirits —has a great deal of power; nor do we need convincing that kings—or, at any rate, Governments—can do a great deal; nor do we need convincing of the power of women.

* 1 Esdras iv. 41.

But we do need to remind ourselves of the social power of accepted truths. Great is the truth, and prevails.

Read the early chapters of the Acts — those early chapters which Thomas Carlyle contrasts in their effective brevity with the wordy volumes of the French political philosopher. Read those few chapters with their fascinating account of the early Christian community. Why did they live so effectively, so socially, so fraternally, so as to irresistibly attract men and women to join them? Because they believed religious truths in common and with all their hearts: they 'continued steadfastly in the Apostles' doctrine'; they had, in other words, a creed, or accepted dogmas.

Thus, they believed that GOD was their FATHER; that He had given His SON in their nature to redeem them; that He had sent His HOLY SPIRIT to dwell in their hearts and to give them both knowledge of His Name and power in human life; that they had been born again in Holy Baptism, and were fed in Holy Communion all together, as brothers in one common family, with the Divine and human life of the Son of Man. These were their dogmas. They are still ours. They are called the doctrines of the Holy TRINITY, of the Incarnation, the Atonement, the Sacraments, the Church.

Will you give your attention to such a short account as you will find in this book of these and such-like fundamental truths of the Christian religion?

If I can help any men or women to see the meaning of these dogmas—(1) that they are true and can be proclaimed on reasonable grounds; (2) that they have a direct application in human life; (3) that they should commend themselves to a (good) man's conscience—I am sure I shall have done them a service.

For we need accepted religious truths—that is, dogmas —to give power to our common life.

THE FATHERHOOD OF GOD

' I say to thee, do thou repeat
To the first man thou mayest meet
In lane, highway, or open street—
That he and we and all men move
Under a canopy of love
As broad as the blue sky above.

*　　　*　　　*　　　*　　　*

That we on divers shores now cast
Shall meet, our perilous voyage past,
All in our FATHER'S house at last.'

ONE elementary dogma of the Christian religion is the
Fatherhood of GOD. In popular idea it is the very
opposite of a dogma. Nothing seems less to savour of
' dogmatic religion ' than the truth that GOD is our
FATHER, and all we are brethren. For the present, however, we will leave aside the question whether or not it
is a dogmatic truth, and betake ourselves to the consideration of its meaning. For, in fact, though it seems
the most familiar idea, and the most certainly Christian,
Christian people are very often found to be sadly puzzled
as to its real meaning. In part this is due to the influence in England of the great but misleading teacher
Calvin, of Geneva, who led people to believe that multitudes of human beings are from the moment of their
creation appointed by the absolute will of GOD to ever-
lasting condemnation. In part, on the other hand, it is
due to the loose and unscriptural notions of those who
are sometimes called Latitudinarians, who would rob the
doctrine of GOD's Fatherhood of all its severity.

Now, in a certain sense the Fatherhood of GOD or gods

is a truth held in almost all religions. All men tend to believe that they derive their life from their god. St. Paul could quote the Greek poet to the Athenians as saying that 'we are all the offspring of GOD'*—that is to say, that GOD is the FATHER of all men. But that we derive our life from GOD—though, in a sense, it leads on to all else—is by itself but a little part of what Christians mean by His Fatherhood.

I.

By GOD's Fatherhood we mean His impartial love. Back behind all in this world, which seems so cruel, so unjust, so unequal, Christians believe there beats the heart of a FATHER, a heart of impartial love. This truth is constantly stated or implied in the New Testament: 'GOD is love,' and 'With GOD is no respect of persons.' 'Ye call on the FATHER, who, without respect of persons, judgeth according to every man's work.'† A very pleasant idea, this impartial love of GOD—we sometimes feel inclined to say—but it is contrary to plain facts. One man is much tempted; another, hardly at all. One man has every kind of advantage in life; another, every drawback. One man knows the whole Christian truth; another is in what is called 'heathen darkness.' And yet it is supposed that the Christian faith is necessary to salvation. Is all this justice? Is all this impartial love?

Well, I will not examine this sort of objection in detail, but I will take it as it stands.

Nor will I discuss for the moment why there should be all this inequality among men, or to what extent it is GOD's will, and to what extent, on the other hand, man's sin has brought it about. But, taking all the manifest inequality of the world as it stands, I ask, does it contradict the idea of GOD's impartial love? No, it does not; because GOD views each man and judges him in the

* Acts xvii. 28 29.
† 1 St. John iv. 8; Acts x. 34; 1 St. Pet. i. 17.

light of all his advantages and disadvantages. He thinks a good deal of kind words from one whose temper is naturally irritable, and very little of the same words from one who finds it easy to be pleasant. He makes light of the temperance of a respectable gentleman who would shiver at the bare idea of being drunk, but He highly esteems the temperance of one whose circumstances are full of temptations to drink. In a word, in forming His estimate of us, GOD never forgets what our natures and opportunities are, and He judges us according to them.

No doubt, one reason why our nature and our opportunities are so unequal is because of the Divine system of election—that is, because GOD chooses special people for special privileges. But does this election mean favouritism? Most certainly not. The Jews were the ' elect' among all the ancient nations for the knowledge of the true GOD, but did this mean they were ' favourites'? Hear the prophets repudiate the idea. 'You only,' says GOD by the mouth of Amos—' You only have I known of all the families of the earth: therefore will I visit upon you all your iniquities.'* This is a truth of which the Old and New Testaments are full, and a truth which the elect are sadly unwilling to learn—that in proportion to our election is our responsibility. One man is elect to riches, another to some special power, such as the gift of ready speech or of singing, another to a good natural disposition, others (as Christians) to the true knowledge of GOD in CHRIST. And each sort of election brings its corresponding responsibility. On the other hand, no man is responsible for any truth or gift which has not been entrusted to him. The heathen, for instance, who have not known the Gospel, are not responsible for their ignorance of it. GOD is a FATHER—a FATHER of impartial love. He ' will have all men to be saved,' and we can be quite certain that none will fall short of salvation for any deficiency in capacity or in opportunity. GOD'S

* Amos iii. 2.

Fatherhood means this *impartial* love, and He has eternity to work in to fill up to the full measure of satisfaction those natures which in this life have seemed to have but poor chances, yet have made the best of the chances they had.

II.

GOD's Fatherhood means His individual love. With GOD every man counts for one, and nobody counts for more than one. This does not mean that all men are meant to be equal in position, for we are naturally unequal in capacity; so much so that, as we are often told, if we were all made equal in position on Monday morning, we should be unequal again by Saturday night. But it does mean that all men are equally valuable in GOD's sight, and that He wills that everyone should have a real opportunity of making the best of himself. In GOD's sight no man is lost in the crowd, and GOD, who can see what goes on in each man's heart, has eternity to carry out His Divine designs. This is a truth which in this disordered and crowded world it is difficult to keep in mind. GOD really loves each man, as if there were none other in the world to love. 'Say not thou in thine heart, I shall not be remembered from above: for what am I among so many people, and what is my soul among such an infinite number of creatures?'* GOD creates and loves, and has His eye on, not all only, but each. Does it seem impossible to believe this? Think, then, how in our own case, as knowledge advances and broadens, it becomes also less vague or general, and more particular. The schoolmaster knows his boys better than a stranger. That is, he knows them more particularly. So it is with action. The good surgeon, for instance, differs from the bad surgeon, because he acts less by mere general rules, and with more individual insight into particular cases. Carry his thought up and apply it to the perfect GOD. GOD's

---

* Ecclus. xvi. 17.

perfection means that the universal range and scope of the
Divine knowledge and operations, as over all creatures
whatsoever, diminishes nothing from their particular application. GOD knows you and me, and acts upon you and
me, as if there were none other in the world for Him to
know and act upon. And this truth of GOD's individual
love JESUS CHRIST specially connects with His Name of
FATHER.*

For all that a Calvin may have said, then, GOD's
Fatherhood means His impartial and individual love for
every human being.

III.

But it means also His jealous love—for all that Latitudinarians may say.

Jealousy is mostly used in a bad sense, of the exaggerated
claims which one man may make on another—husband
on wife, friend on friend. But there is a right sort of
jealousy, a more or less exclusive claim of a right sort—
such, for instance, as a husband makes on a wife, a wife
on a husband, a father on a child. Thus, GOD is a
jealous GOD, because, as *the* FATHER of spirits, He must
make the claim of a father on the hearts of his children.
' If I be a FATHER, where is Mine honour?' Yes, if GOD
were our Maker only, He might be satisfied with an
external service and a routine of observance. But because
He is our FATHER He cannot be satisfied without finding
in us the response of sons. According to our opportunities,
no doubt, is His demand; but according to our opportunities the demand is certainly made, and is inexorable.

Milk-and-water Christianity forgets this. But it makes
itself heard in all the tremendous sternness of the Son
of Man. We are made for sonship. Sonship is union of
heart and life and mind. GOD seeks in us a desire for
His fellowship corresponding to His offer of love. And
because GOD is a FATHER, and unchangeably a FATHER,

---

* *E.g.*, St. Matt. x. 29, 30.

therefore He must be wrathful, with an unalterable anger, against sons who will not behave towards Him like sons. Do not let us forget that GOD is not less awful because He is a FATHER.

IV.

It follows from this that GOD must punish us when we sin against Him—that His Fatherhood means not only love, but discipline. 'If we are without chastisement, whereof all are partakers, then are we bastards, and not sons.'* We are not yet going to consider anything so difficult as the origin of sin, or the terrible hold which it has got on human hearts and on the world. But the existence of sin is a fact of experience, and it is a fact of experience, also, that not without suffering are men cleansed from it—that there is no purgatory without pain, whether in this life or beyond it. Thus, our FATHER is a GOD of discipline. 'He scourgeth every son whom He receiveth,' even as the 'beloved SON' was the 'Man of Sorrows.'

V.

GOD's Fatherhood means, indeed, an infinite readiness to forgive. There is no limit to the number of times that GOD will accept our imperfect repentances, and encourage us to begin afresh. As long as we are capable of returning to choose GOD, GOD is assuredly willing to receive us. But all the same, we cannot fail to see that the FATHER may be finally driven to reject His sons. We can be sure that every man will have the fullest opportunity of knowing GOD, and making his peace with Him in this life or beyond it. But supposing a man has gone on refusing opportunities, and sinning against his light till he has finally destroyed all the good that was in him, and taken evil to be his good and Satan to be his god . . . what can be his last end but to be banished from the

* Heb. xii. 5.

presence of his FATHER? This is a terrible thought to which we shall have to return. Meanwhile let us be content to have thought for awhile together of the simplest of Christian truths—the Fatherhood of GOD; for, simple as the truth is, experience shows that Christian people prove very often strangely ignorant of its meaning.

Does it not make all the difference in the world to us if we really believe that we have a Heavenly FATHER? If we really know that the Almighty Governor of the whole world is not a tyrant, but a FATHER who overlooks no soul that He has created, but attends to each and cares for each, and claims the love and service of each impartially and individually; and who, if for a while He hides His face from us and disciplines us with sharp punishment, will certainly at the last give us the fullest measure of satisfaction of which we are capable—if we know this, I say, may not we feel the sun always shining in our hearts?

WHAT ARE CHRISTIAN DOGMAS?

> ' And so the Word had breath, and wrought
> With human hands the creed of creeds
> In loveliness of perfect deeds,
> More strong than all poetic thought.'

IT surprises people to be told that the Fatherhood of GOD is a Christian dogma. They think that it belongs to ' undogmatic religion.' I suppose they imagine that a truth cannot be a dogma unless it has an unpleasant sound. But a Christian dogma does not mean an unpleasant truth, but a truth which everyone who would be a Christian is bound to believe—a truth accepted by Christians, without question, as a starting-point for their life and work. And the Fatherhood of GOD is one of these accepted Christian truths. People who are not Christians may borrow it and hold it, for it finds an echo in every heart—' the testimony of the soul naturally Christian '—yet, in historical fact, it came into the world as a part of Christianity—in the sense, at least, in which I tried to explain it in the last chapter.

More than this, it is a Christian dogma, because no one has real grounds for believing it certainly and securely but one who recognises that CHRIST is GOD and that He rose from the dead. For however obvious it seems, when life smiles upon us, that GOD is our FATHER, it is in fact very difficult to believe it when the spectacle of pain and failure is all around us, and our mind is filled by it. Then the Fatherhood of GOD seems an idea contradicted by experience, an idea which Nature scouts and turns to ridicule.

How did CHRIST make it credible? Not by explaining the mystery of pain, for He gave not one word of explanation, but by revealing the love of GOD *in* pain and *through* pain. If some bright angel had come down from heaven with a message that ' GOD is love,' we could not have believed it. We should have said: ' These are fine words, but we know the facts, and the facts of experience contradict this fine message.' Only the Man of Sorrows could have made us believe that it is true.

And if He had been mere man He would not have proved its truth. He would only have been one of many martyrs, and it would have been no proof of Divine Fatherhood that the best of men, after a life of suffering and rejection, should have been harried to death on Calvary. But CHRIST claimed to be the SON of GOD, one with the FATHER in spirit and mind and being. His love is therefore GOD's love. It was no one else than the very SON of GOD who took our nature, entered into our pain, and clothed Himself in all the unmerited suffering and failure and ignominy which seems such an argument against the Divine love. Out of the very heart of pain and failure He manifested that self-sacrificing love which is nothing else than GOD's love, and, by His resurrection on the third day from the dead, finally proved the Divine love triumphant through pain and over pain.

Henceforth men have not indeed a clear, logical account to give of the meaning of suffering, and why it is allowed in GOD's world. Pain still remains a mystery. But they have something better than an explanation. They have facts. If JESUS of Nazareth is indeed the SON of GOD made man, and if He rose from the dead, then it is quite certain and plain to all men (1) that GOD is a loving FATHER; (2) that through all pain and failure the purpose of GOD st works on to its triumphant issue, as CHRIST, seemingly defeated in death, rose again the third day from the dead, King of kings and Lord of lords.

This is what I mean when I say that, in order to have a real reason for believing securely and certainly that GOD is our FATHER, in spite of the pain of which the world is full, we must believe that JESUS is SON of GOD, and is risen from the dead.

Now you will understand why I call the Fatherhood of GOD a Christian dogma. Now, also, I can explain briefly, and once for all, what is the ground of all Christian dogmas. They are simply those truths which a man must hold if he is to share the life which CHRIST brought into the world, and if he is to have fellowship in the faith, the hope, the love, which He made possible. This faith, hope and love, this Christian life, is based on truths which were imparted to men, or confirmed to them, by JESUS CHRIST in His example and in His teaching. This life, with the truths on which it rests, was committed by CHRIST to His Apostles, and through them to the visible society or Church which is to represent Him in the world until the end. Christian dogmas, then, are simply statements of those truths which are the necessary background or basis of the Christian life.

For their justification we make appeal in part to experience past and present—to the life which, in fact, has been lived ever since the beginning of Christianity by those who have *really* believed these truths. We ask men to pay attention, and see what peace, what strength, what hope, what love, has come of believing. Can such a beautiful and constant result be due to anything else than that these truly Christian men and women have got at the secret of human life, and have power to live noble lives because they have a hold on eternal truth? But we appeal also to history—to the Gospels, which tell us of what CHRIST was, what He claimed to be; how He lived, and suffered, and taught, and died, and rose again, and reigns for ever: and to Apostolic Epistles and Acts, which tell us how His first disciples thought of Him. That we have very good reason for believing that these documents are genuine, and contain authentic history, I am sure. I am sure, also, that anyone who studies them as impartially as he would study ordinary history will come to this conclusion also. But at present I am concerned, not with justifying the Christian dogmas, but only with explaining them. So, if you please, I will go on to interpret, as best I can, the doctrines of our religion, and to show you how close a bearing they have on common human life.

A DIALOGUE ON THE HOLY TRINITY

> ' When heaven and earth were yet unmade,
>   When time was yet unknown,
> Thou, in Thy bliss and majesty,
>   Didst live and love alone.
>
> ' Most ancient of all mysteries !
>   Before Thy Throne we lie ;
> Have mercy now, most Merciful,
>   Most Holy TRINITY.'

I WAS walking out on Sunday, when I was joined by my friend Mr. Plainman, and we took a walk together. He told me he had been reading the earlier chapters of this little book in the form in which they originally appeared in *Goodwill,* and had learned that I was preparing to write about the doctrine of the Holy TRINITY.

' You will be clever,' he added, ' if you make *that* credible to a man of my sort. I went to church on Trinity Sunday to hear Canon Wakemall preach ; but long before we got to the sermon I had lost my temper, I can tell you, over the Athanasian Creed. " *The FATHER is GOD, the SON is GOD, and the HOLY GHOST is GOD ; and yet they are not three GODS, but one GOD.*" This seems to me little better than nonsense, and contrary to what we used to learn when we did addition sums together at school. So last Sunday I went to the Unitarian Chapel, and I heard a sermon there about the Fatherhood of GOD which seemed to me full of a practical sort of religion. Why can't we be satisfied with believing, like the Unitarians, in one GOD, our Creator and our FATHER, without adding on to this a doctrine of the TRINITY, which seems to insult one's common-sense?'

'Well,' I said, 'but supposing we haven't "added on" anything to the belief in one GOD, our Creator and our FATHER: what then? You were good enough to say you had read some of these papers of mine on Christian doctrines. Did you read what I said about the Father-hood of GOD?'

'Yes, I did,' he said; 'but my mind is like a sieve for these religious discussions. I can't keep hold of them. However, I believe what you said was that, with all the evil and misery in the world, men would not have been able to believe in the Fatherhood of GOD, meaning His love, without the revelation of it given by JESUS CHRIST. I must admit I think there is truth in that. You know how my Mary has been trying to comfort our poor neighbour whose wife has just died with her first child. She has been trying to persuade the poor, heart-broken, despairing fellow of the love of GOD. But she said, truly enough, that one could not have the face to mention Divine love in the neighbourhood of such agony as his, if it were not the Man of Sorrows who assured us of it.'

'Well,' I said, 'if you are disposed to grant that CHRIST's love is GOD's love—that is, that CHRIST is really the SON of the FATHER in Heaven, sent to reveal His character in our human nature—I shall not have much more to persuade you of, for you can hardly then doubt the doctrine of the TRINITY.'

'I *am* disposed to grant that,' he said—'at any rate, for the moment and for the sake of argument. But does it carry me all the way you think?'

'Yes,' I said; 'the doctrine of the TRINITY is only putting into a short formula what is implied in all our LORD's language about His own relation to the FATHER, who sent Him, and the SPIRIT, whom the FATHER and He were to send to accomplish His work. You are fond of climbing mountains, and you know how a surface of rock, which looks flat and uniform from a distance, seems broken up and complicated enough as you get near to it. So, as we got nearer to GOD, or, rather, as He came nearer to us, the distinctions in His nature began to come out. Seen from a distance, as in the Old Testament, He seemed merely one and single. As He came nearer to us in the coming of the SON and the SPIRIT, we grew to see that the one GOD is manifold as well as one. There is a FATHER sending, and a SON sent to reveal Him, and a SPIRIT proceeding from Him to give life. So it is that the one Name of the LORD GOD becomes the Name of the FATHER, and the SON, and the HOLY SPIRIT. It is only GOD coming nearer to us, so that we see more distinctly the relationships in which His being consists. It is only to put this in other words to say that the Apostles, in coming to know GOD more familiarly through CHRIST, came to believe in FATHER and SON and SPIRIT as part of their experience. They had come to know GOD to be FATHER through their fellowship with the SON, and by the power of the SPIRIT which had come upon them. All that the Church did after this was to put this revelation into a short formula, which should express and protect the truth about GOD which had been received from the Apostles.'

' But how,' asked my friend, ' can a doctrine be revealed truth when it seems to be nonsense ? How can three Persons be one GOD ? If the FATHER is GOD, the SON is GOD, and the HOLY GHOST is GOD, here then, are three GODS, according to the law of simple addition !'

' I do not think it would become a thoughtful man,' I replied, ' to reject the doctrine of the TRINITY on *this* ground. At any rate, Professor Huxley would not allow you to. He once said as much in a private letter which he gave me leave to quote; and I learned his words by heart, for I thought they might be useful. "I have not," he said, "the slightest objection to offer *a priori* [that is,

on grounds of reason] to all the propositions of the three
Creeds. The mysteries of the Church are child's play
compared with the mysteries of Nature. The doctrine
of the TRINITY is not more puzzling than the necessary
antinomies [that is, contradictions] of physical nature."*
I am sure, my good friend, if you read what any scientific
writer says about the ether which is the vehicle of light
and heat, you will find it all " metaphysical " and " incomprehensible " enough.

'This ether is described to us by physicists as diffused
through all space; but though it is everywhere, it cannot
be discovered anywhere, and when its properties are
examined it seems to be at once a solid and a fluid. This
is mysterious indeed, and passes our limited power of
imagination; but, nevertheless, it appears to be true, and
is regarded as true by the scientific world.

'Or, again, have you ever thought steadily about your
own inner self, with its will and reason and feelings? Do
you not know how your feelings often go against your
will or your reason; or, again, your reason against your
feeling and your will? They seem very distinct, these
parts of your nature. They are plainly three different
things. But yet, for all their distinctness, your inner self
is one. You are one being, not many. Even this consideration of your own nature may teach you that what is
one may be at the same time also three.'

'Do you mean that a man like Huxley would tell me it
is reasonable to believe that one GOD is three Persons?'

'Huxley would recognise,' I replied, 'that the primary
elements of nature are mysterious, that human language
can express them very imperfectly, and that even human
thought finds itself baffled to *conceive* about them what
still it must *believe*. In regard to the nature of GOD, the
Christian Church was compelled by its experience of
CHRIST to believe that in the unity of the one GOD is
the FATHER, the SON, and the HOLY SPIRIT; and she

* Quoted in Bampton Lecture, 1891 (Murray), p. 296.

chose gradually, with much hesitation and many apologies, the best words she could find to express the mysterious truth.'

' But, at least,' he said, ' you will admit that, if the doctrine of the TRINITY is a real revelation, it is a quite unpractical truth, and one which it would be as well to keep out of sight as much as possible.'

' I admit nothing of the kind,' I replied—' quite the contrary. It is only the belief in the TRINITY which enables one to think about GOD at all, or to worship Him with any degree of intelligence and satisfaction.'

' Don't be paradoxical,' he said.

' What I said may be paradoxical or not,' I made rejoinder, ' but it is true. Your Unitarian friend would tell you, would he not, to believe in and to worship one eternal GOD, who is one without any distinction of Persons ? Well now, I say, how can I think of such a GOD as a living or loving Being in Himself at all ? This Unitarian GOD is a mere First Cause, or supreme point of government, without life and love in His own being.'

' What do you mean ?' he said.

' Do you admit,' I asked, ' that GOD existed before all creation a living, loving GOD ?'

' Yes,' he said ; ' I suppose all believers in GOD admit as much as this.'

' Well, then,' I went on, ' how can there be life without productiveness, or love without someone to love ? If GOD is eternally alive, He must have been eternally productive, eternally fruitful. If he was eternally loving, there must have been an eternal object of His love. Now, little as we can penetrate into the depths of the being of GOD, if we believe in the TRINITY, we can at least perceive that GOD was eternally alive, eternally moving, eternally productive. The FATHER was ever expressing Himself in His " Word," or " Image," or " SON," and the FATHER and the SON together were having fellowship in the SPIRIT of Life, the product and the joy of both.

GOD is one, but in this unity there is productiveness and fellowship, and therefore life and love. GOD is mysterious, no doubt, but in that mystery there is something intelligible, something akin to ourselves. We know what life is in our own case; we know that our life is only possible because we can express ourselves in what we say, or do, or produce, and because we can think about some object and love some other. Life is fruitful and social, and must be fruitful and social if it is to be life at all. Thus, it is as social beings, as operative or fruitful beings, that we are made in the image of GOD, because GOD is in Himself productive and social—GOD in the fellowship of His eternal being: FATHER, SON, and HOLY SPIRIT. GOD *is* love. We cannot, again be it said, explain GOD. The depths of GOD are unsearchable. We must mostly be silent and adore. But at least the one GOD in TRINITY is a mystery full of warmth, and life, and comfort. The mystery of the Unitarian's GOD is something unintelligible; something which sheds no light on our human life, which helps us in no way to understand how human life, social and fruitful, is made in the image of the eternal life of GOD.'

'I always thought,' he said, 'that it was only the spirit or mind of man that was made in GOD's image.'

'No,' I replied; 'it is man altogether—man as a social being in the family, the State, the Church—that reflects GOD's life and is made in His image.'

There was silence awhile, and as my friend was turning to go home, I said: 'Have I persuaded you that the doctrine of the TRINITY is full of meaning for human life?'

'I don't know,' he said; 'these things are puzzling. I can't keep theological arguments in my head. But I will tell you what I will do: I will read some of the Gospels and attend to CHRIST's language about Himself, and the FATHER, and the SPIRIT. I can't say I am convinced at present.'

And with that I had to be content. I consoled myself

by reflecting that he was more likely to be brought to worship GOD by the study of the Gospels than by any words of mine; and to worship is certainly the way to know. But I determined that our argument should be written down for my readers to judge whether I am not right in what I maintained : (1) that the doctrine of the TRINITY is only the putting into such words as we can utter of what was disclosed about GOD when He came near to men in the appearing of the CHRIST and the mission of the HOLY SPIRIT ; * (2) that the doctrine of the Holy TRINITY—that is, the doctrine that GOD is in Himself eternally productive, social, operative—helps us both to think about Him and to worship Him with intelligence, and enables us to recognise that human life can be in His image only by becoming continually more operative, more fruitful, more social.

* See, for example, St. Matt. xi. 27, xii. 32, xxviii. 19 ; and St. John xiv.

REVELATION, OR THE WORD OF GOD

' Strong SON of GOD, immortal Love,
    Whom we, that have not seen Thy face,
    By faith, and faith alone, embrace,
Believing where we cannot prove :

Thine are these orbs of light and shade ;
    Thou madest Life in man and brute ;
    Thou madest Death ; and, lo ! Thy foot
Is on the skull that Thou hast made.

' Thou wilt not leave us in the dust ;
    Thou madest man, he knows not why ;
    He thinks he was not made to die ;
And Thou hast made him : Thou art just.

' Thou seemest human and Divine,
    The highest, holiest manhood Thou :
    Our wills are ours, we know not how ;
Our wills are ours, to make them Thine.

' Our little systems have their day ;
    They have their day, and cease to be :
    They are but broken lights of Thee,
And Thou, O LORD, art more than they.'

I HAVE been trying to explain part of the Christian creed,
and more of it I am to go on to explain. And my reason
for doing so is that here is the light to live by and the
power to make men free. But the Christian creed is only
light and power when it is accepted as the Word of GOD,
as the truth divinely revealed, the one religion of redemption for struggling, sinning men. Now, a good number of
people in our time stumble at this notion of one revealed
religion. ' There are so many religions in the world,' they
say ; ' is it likely that one will be true and the rest false ?
We quite admit that it gives a man great courage and

27

power in life to believe in "one Name under heaven whereby men must be saved," but it is after all only a narrow fanaticism.'

Who has not heard some traveller, who has assisted at the worship of different sorts of Christians, and witnessed the religious devotion of Mohammedans and Hindus and Buddhists, use this sort of language?

Let it be admitted then that there have been, and are, narrow and fanatical Christians—and there are, be it remembered, other vices in the world besides narrowness and fanaticism—but the notion of the ' one religion ' is not itself narrow ; it is compatible with the largest-hearted and most liberal reason.   Let us think.

It is certainly a truth of the Bible that GOD is revealed everywhere and in all things.   Nature is nothing else but a gradual disclosure of His power, His order, His beauty. ' The invisible things of Him from the creation of the world are clearly seen, being understood by the things that are made, even His eternal power and Godhead,'* so wrote St. Paul.   ' There is no creature so small and common but shows us the goodness of GOD,' says the author of ' The Imitation of Christ.'   Once more, there is a further revelation of GOD in humanity.   The more truly human men are, the more they recognise as binding on them a law of righteousness; and the more men are conscious of their individuality, the more they learn that the dignity of each single soul lies in obedience to this law.   Here then, in the human conscience all over the world, is to be found, more or less, a revelation of the Divine righteousness.   On this point also let us hear St. Paul.   ' When the Gentiles, which have not the law [*i.e.*, the heathen who have no special ' law ' such as was given to the Jews] do by nature the things contained in the law, these, having not the law, are a law unto themselves; which show the work of the law written in their hearts, their conscience bearing witness, and their mutual reasonings accusing

* Rom. i. 20.

or else excusing one another.'* This is the universal revelation of conscience. And beside this there is the revelation through prophets. There are men who feel beyond their fellows some truth of GOD, and, feeling it, proclaim it, and, finding response in the duller consciences of their fellow-men, are recognised as revealers of the light, to be honoured and obeyed. This spirit of prophecy is to found among heathen peoples—in a Zoroaster, a Buddha, an Æschylus; and St. Paul seems to recognise it there, for he quotes to the Athenians a heathen poet, and calls a Cretan poet a 'prophet of their own.'† But that which existed as scattered sparks among all nations was as an ever clearer burning light among the Jews. Men who are not orthodox Christians, yet recognise that it was given to the Jews to have a pre-eminent consciousness of GOD. Among them was what an old Father called 'the sacred school of the knowledge of GOD and of the spiritual life for all mankind.' And the light of this clearer revelation, given 'in many parts and many manners,'‡ came at last to its climax and fulfilment in 'the Light of the World,' JESUS CHRIST, the very SON of GOD incarnate. It was all one process. He, the Word of GOD, was always speaking—everywhere and at all times. He 'was coming into the world.' But at the end of the long process He was not 'coming,' but 'come.' The true Light shone, and henceforward it 'lightens every man' of all ages and nations and classes who will come to receive it.§

Now, this is no narrow creed. Christianity, the religion of JESUS, is the Light; it is the one final Revelation, the one final Religion; but it supersedes all other religions, Jewish and pagan, not by *excluding*, but by *including* all the elements of truth which each contained. There was light in Zoroastrianism, light in Buddhism, light among the Greeks; but it is all included in Christianity. A good Christian is a good Buddhist, a good Jew, a good Moham-

* Rom. ii. 14, 15.   † Acts xvii. 28 ; Titus i. 12.
‡ Heb. i. 1.   § See St. John i. 1-18.

medan, a good Zoroastrian; that is, he has all the truth and virtue that these can possess, purged and fused in a greater and completer light. Christianity, I say, supersedes all other religions by including their fragments of truth in its own completeness. You cannot show me any element of spiritual light or strength which is in other religions and is not in Christianity. Nor can you show me any other religion which can compare with Christianity in completeness of light. Christianity is the one complete and final religion, and the elements of truth in other religions are rays of the One Light which is concentrated and shines full in JESUS CHRIST our LORD.

And it all came about, this one continuous revelation of GOD, in the way which accords with human experience in other departments. The good things occur first in some one place or time, where the conditions are suitable for their appearance. Then they spread from a centre, by means natural and artificial, over the surface of the earth. The potato plant is good for all men. But it was discovered in some one district, and then spread, as occasion served, to accommodate all men. So it is with great thoughts and inventions. So it is with religion. All the distinct belief in one GOD which now exists has spread from the faith of Abraham. And the full faith in GOD Incarnate, in the FATHER, the SON, and the HOLY GHOST, began from Jerusalem, and is still spreading, to be the light and strength of all men. It was welcomed by Jews first, then by Greeks, Romans, Teutons, Celts. It is to be welcomed still by Chinamen, Japanese, Hindus, and races beyond number. It is adapted to all races; and as each race has found in it light and life, so each has brought out something more of its manifold power and meaning. It shows its power, moreover, not at one stage of human progress, but at all. It spread in the Roman Empire. It sanctified the life of the Middle Ages. It gave its impulse to the movements of the Reformation. It is to be the strength of the coming democracy. For all ages and for

all men CHRIST is to be the Light, the one Redeemer and
Emancipator of men. And it is only in all ages and races,
and under all forms of society, that its full power and
meaning can appear. Christianity is still young and
adequate to the future.

And wherever the Christian Revelation comes it comes
with the authority of truth. The utterance of conscience
is always authoritative. Religious truth is always authoritative. It lays its claim on men. At all times and for all
men, under all religions, ' the light which lighteneth every
man ' must be obeyed. Everywhere it is the same GOD,
FATHER, SON, and HOLY GHOST present, even where His
name and nature is not rightly known, present and claim-
ing the allegiance of man. Only, where He is most clearly
revealed, there He speaks with greatest authority. A good
heathen man who is true to his light is always obeying the
word of the one true GOD. But as that word makes itself
more clearly heard, so it must be more diligently obeyed.
And where CHRIST is clearly known as CHRIST, there He
must be obeyed and accepted as CHRIST. The twilight is
better than darkness. But the full light is better than
the twilight; and to refuse the light and choose the twilight
is the same thing as to love the darkness.

This is the meaning of Revelation. This is the doctrine
of the One Religion.

Now, I ask, is not this a reasonable, hopeful doctrine—
much more reasonable, much more hopeful, than the sort of
Latitudinarianism which says, more or less clearly, that all
religions are on a common level of certainty or uncertainty?

This Latitudinarian idea was skilfully expressed by the
German poet Lessing, in the old parable of the three
rings put into the mouth of Nathan the Wise. In the
time of the Crusades, Saladin the Mohammedan is represented as asking Nathan, the wise Jew, how he determined which religion was true—the Jewish, the Christian,
or the Mohammedan; and Nathan replies by a parable. A
certain man had a priceless ring, which had the peculiar

gift of making its wearer acceptable to GOD and man. He
left it to his most dearly beloved son, with the injunction
that he in his turn and each of his successors should leave
it in the same manner to his best beloved son, who should
thereby become the head of the family. The ring passed
on till it came to one who had three sons all equally
beloved. To each in turn he promised the ring. That
none of the three might be disappointed, he had two other
rings made, indistinguishable even by himself from the
original. One of the three he gave to each of the three
sons. Each, after his father's death, claimed to have the
true ring, and accused his brothers of imposture. They
rushed finally before a judge. He should decide among
their claims. ' It is the property of the true ring,' said
the judge, ' to make its owner beloved of GOD and man.
Who is the best beloved of his fellows ?' Alas! no one
of the three was beloved of his fellows. Each was selfish
and lived only for himself. ' Then,' said the judge, ' let
the matter wait for many generations. Let each ring,
believed by its possessor to be the only genuine one, go
down its own line of descent. Let each owner of a ring
strive to make himself beloved for his goodness of all the
others. Then, thousands of years on, a wiser judge than
I shall decide which is the true ring.'

The parable speaks for itself. Nathan means that no
man can decide which is the true religion. No man is
meant to decide it. Perhaps no man will ever be able to.
Meanwhile let each hold to his own religion and do his
best, and the wise man will recognise that the important
matter is, not the creed, but the conduct.

By the mouth of Nathan, Lessing speaks the Latitudinarian opinion. No one religion can make good its special
claim for truth. The important matter is, not what a
man's creed is, but what his conduct is.

Now, there are many fallacies in this opinion. It is,
for example, quite certain that what a man's conduct will
be will depend in the long-run on what his real creed is.

The moral fruits of the Mohammedan creed, for example, are apparent in history, and they are very different from the moral fruits of the Christian creed. Moreover, a religion, to bear its proper fruit at all, must be believed in as *the true religion*. In order to act decisively, we must believe decisively. But I will not now dwell upon this. I would now only ask you to recognise into what a hopeless position this Latitudinarian view puts a man's *reason*. He can really believe his religion only so long as he is ignorant and fanatical. When once he begins to think, all that seemed certain in his mind becomes uncertain. The more wise he becomes, the more vague become his convictions. More wisdom means less knowledge, less certainty, less clearness about GOD or His will. Is this reasonable or encouraging to reason? Is it not far more reasonable to believe that in religion, as elsewhere, there is a possibility of progress in knowledge, a continually clearer light. Every man can know something of GOD, but the gradually growing knowledge of GOD which there has been in the world among Zoroastrians, Buddhists, Greeks, Jews, is come to fulness of knowledge in the revelation of JESUS CHRIST; in Him all the treasures of wisdom and knowledge are hid, and here is for evermore a light full and inexhaustible—a continually developing possibility of clear knowledge of GOD.

Yes, GOD has been everywhere revealing Himself: in Nature, in its power, order, beauty; in man, in his individual and social conscience, in his various sciences, in the movements of human progress; in his prophets, who have received more vividly than others the impression of His glory and His will. In all ways and places GOD has been manifesting Himself, and all these various and complex revelations come to a centre where He, the one true GOD, is personally manifested in a human nature, the human nature of JESUS, very man and very GOD, in whom is the perfect revelation of the FATHER's nature and the perfect revelation of the capacity and dignity of man.

3

THE INCARNATION OF THE SON OF GOD

' He who did most shall bear most; the strongest shall stand the
    most weak;
 'Tis the weakness in strength that I cry for! my flesh that I seek
 In the Godhead! I seek and I find it. Oh, Saul, it shall be
 A Face like my face that receives thee; a Man like to me
 Thou shalt love and be loved by, for ever: a Hand like this hand
 Shall throw open the gate of new life to thee! see the CHRIST
    stand!'

THERE once appeared on our earth, going about doing
good, bearing men's sicknesses and carrying their infirmi-
ties, One, JESUS of Nazareth, true man in all that makes
up human nature, whom those nearest to Him gradually
discovered, by the authority of His words and works, by
the miracles of His love and judgment and by His victory
over death, to be the Eternal SON of GOD. They—His
first disciples—came to believe in His Godhead through
their experience of His manhood; and, coming so to
believe, they handed on their faith as an inheritance to
the Christian Church, an inheritance which the record of
the words and deeds of JESUS of Nazareth, and the per-
petual experience of His power in those who believe, has
made continually more credible.

We of the Christian Church believe, then, that the
Eternal SON or Word of GOD, Himself very GOD, the
Second Person of the Blessed TRINITY, was made very
man by taking flesh of the Virgin Mary, and appeared on
earth as JESUS of Nazareth, to live, and work, and suffer,
and die, and rise again from the dead, and ascend up to
the FATHER's right hand, where He was before.

This dogma will now become the subject for our consideration. It seems to some people hard of belief. But we must never forget that this SON or Word of GOD, who was made man in JESUS CHRIST, was, and is, also present in all His creation and in all His creatures. He was at all times everywhere in the world. He was always manifesting Himself in Nature, in the conscience of men, in the movements of society, in the inspiration of prophets. His delight was always with the sons of men. So that His Incarnation is not an isolated thing—a thing by itself. It is the crown and climax of all that has gone before. He had been gradually becoming more and more powerfully present. He was more present in man than in Nature: more present in prophets than in common men: most of all present when He personally took a human nature in which to show Himself.

This Incarnation is both the disclosure of GOD and the disclosure of our true manhood, and the fresh start for sinful humanity.

1. *The Disclosure of GOD.*—Human nature is so truly made in the image and likeness of GOD, that GOD can really make use of it in order to reveal His own character and person. To understand the nature of GOD by mere thought or argument is difficult or impossible. But we can be taught by an object-lesson. The life of JESUS CHRIST is an object-lesson about GOD. We observe His human love, and authority, and power, and judgment, in His words and in His works; and we know that this human character is the character of very GOD, who has shown Himself to us in the intelligible, unmistakable forms of our own nature. What GOD's justice, mercy, considerateness, severity, mean we can clearly understand by the human justice, mercy, considerateness, severity, of JESUS, who, very man, is also very GOD.

2. *The Disclosure of Man.*—What is the true nature of manhood? What is it to be a real man or woman? How are we to judge? We look around and within, and we

3—2

see a very mixed scene of goodness and badness, love and selfishness, mercy and cruelty, justice and corruption, strength and weakness, purity and uncleanness. Sometimes the bad side of human nature seems so masterful that men have come to the conclusion that human nature is necessarily selfish, and lustful, and cruel, and corrupt. The conscience of mankind has protested against such an idea; but where shall we find a human nature which does not fail us somewhere? Is man then a thing made up necessarily of good and evil? Can there be such a thing as a simply good man? Is there any standard by which to judge what belongs to man, and what is simply the corruption or spoiling of his nature? Yes, there is. JESUS of Nazareth is very man. So truly was man made in GOD's image that GOD could, not merely take a human nature to be, as it were, the veil of His Godhead, but really live a human life without ceasing to be GOD. He was born as man; He grew in body and mind and character as men grow; He was tempted and resisted as man; He believed, and hoped, and feared, and prayed as man; He was in all points tempted like as we are; He was made in all things like unto His brethren, except sin. Thus, in Him we see what man's nature was meant to be. Sin is not truly part of it, but the weakening, the spoiling, the corruption of it. Here is One without alloy of selfishness, or impurity, or cruelty, and, for all that, true and real man; One in whom all men *and women* can find a human nature completely satisfactory, a human nature which sets the standard, a human nature which shows the real glory of mankind, the human nature of the Son of Man.

3. *The Fresh Start for Humanity.*—He was in all points like as we are, except sin. But, ah, what a difference that makes! Philosophers and reformers who have looked below the surface of life and politics have always demanded a fresh start for humanity. Plato, the Greek, long ago said there could be no real remedy for the evils

of society unless you could make a fresh start. He demanded a blank tablet to draw the lineaments of human life afresh. Centuries later Thomas Carlyle, in the generation behind our own, scoffed at the Radicals of his day, who seemed to think that a number of legislative reforms and 'remedial measures' would set human life straight. Nay, he jeered, these are but quack medicines—'Morison's pills.' You need something more radical than your radical measures. Radical means what goes to the root. You want a change at the root of human life—a fundamental change!

Ay, but sin is so ingrained into our nature, it passes on from father to son. How can there be a radical change? How can we renew the roots of our nature? How can we have a new manhood? In fact, we cannot, except in JESUS CHRIST. He alone is the New Man; He alone is Man without sin. From Him alone is there new birth. He alone can give, in truth and reality, what Plato and Carlyle demanded. Born of a Virgin, a new creation, true man, but new man, He only can give us human nature without sin. 'He taketh away the sin of the world.'

But what is sin, and how does He take it away? Ah! this is a big question, but we have all of us the most practical and direct interest in trying to arrive at the answer.

SIN AND REDEMPTION

' Thy spirit weighs the sins of men,
  Thy science fathoms all their guilt ;
Thou sickenest heavily at Thy heart,
  And the pores open—blood is spilt.

     *   *   *   *

And Thou hast shuddered at each act,
  And shrunk with an astonished fear
As if Thou couldst not bear to see
  The loathsomeness of sin so near.'

THE language and work of JESUS CHRIST is full of the
thought that mankind needs a fresh start, a new birth ;
or, in other words, that mankind needs not merely to
progress and be enlightened, but to be redeemed—that is,
bought back out of the slavery of sin.

What is sin ?

There are people who tell us that all that human nature
needs is enlightenment. The only real evil is ignorance.
This was the opinion of the wise Greek Socrates ; and
from the way people talk of ' education ' and ' culture,' as
if it would remove all the troubles of life, you would suppose that many people now hold this same opinion. But
it is false and repugnant to the plain facts. Of course,
there is a great deal of ignorance in the world, and many
of the wrong things that are done are done in mere ignorance—ignorance that is hardly, if at all, culpable. Thus,
truer knowledge would remove a great deal of the evil of
the world, and the man is a fool who makes light of the
value of good education. For example, years ago there
was a great deal of religious persecution : Catholics would
burn Protestants, and Protestants Catholics, and think

that they were doing GOD service. This, we may say, was due largely to ignorance. It needed only knowledge of the true principles of our religion to let good men see that such a way of dealing with religious opinions, which they believed to be wrong, was not at all the way of our LORD. Thus, ignorance, I say, is the source of a great deal of evil, and good education will do away with this. But it will not get to the root of the matter. Sin is not ignorance.

Once again, there is in the world, beyond all question, a great deal of moral poverty and weakness of nature. Men are born with some moral disease, some criminal tendency, some weakness of will. This is a question of more or less : for all men are by nature more or less inclined to evil in some form or another. This is what is called 'original sin.' It is the inherited result of the wrong-doing, the weakness and wilfulness and ignorance, of those who have gone before us, back to the very beginning of our race. This fault or taint of our nature belongs to sin, and is the result of sin. But in the sense in which sin means personal guilt it is not sin of our own, for it is not our own *fault*. It belongs to the materials with which nature supplies us—the 'raw material' we have to work with. It only becomes our fault when we give way to it and adopt it, or fail to take measures to resist it.

Sin proper is our own fault. It is, as St. John says, lawlessness.* There is in the world no sin but lawlessness, and no lawlessness but sin. Everywhere in Nature is the reign of law. The stars and planets in the solar systems move on their appointed courses ; the forces of heat and light and electricity, the various forms of motion, go on each invariably by its own law ; the life of each plant or body develops or fails according to law ; law reigns over the development of all human faculties and powers. But . . . at the centre of man's being there is

* I St. John iii. 4.

a mystery. Man is a moral and not merely a physical being. He can serve with a free service as lawfully as stars or dumb animals, and by his free choice. But he can also rebel. He can know the right and choose the wrong. He may be perfectly enlightened and yet wicked. He may set himself against GOD, against duty, against law. This is sin in its proper sense. Sin is lawlessness. Sin can, within limits, disturb and disorder GOD's world. I say within limits, for man is not GOD, and GOD has not let go out of His hand the government of the world. In the end the universe will reach the end GOD intended for it. The kingdom of GOD will come. But, by the way, and (so to speak) down to a certain depth, man can disturb the order of GOD. He can introduce, he has introduced, lawlessness into the world.

Look at society now! Is it as GOD intended? No. GOD never intended the lust, the selfishness, the cruelty, the godlessness, which curse society to-day. The life of our big cities, the life of our country places, is a parody of GOD's intention.

> ' Never did any public misery
> Rise of itself ; GOD's plagues are grounded still
> On common stains of our humanity.
> And to the flame that ruineth mankind,
> Man gives the matter—or at least gives wind.'

Or look back to primitive man. You see him dimly, in the mist of the past, in a state of savagery. Was that GOD's intention? No; no more than the present condition of civilised man. It was a parody of primitive simplicity, just as our present civilisation is a parody of true civilisation.

It has sometimes been said that there is a conflict between religion and science, because, according to science, man begins at the bottom, and gradually improves ; according to religion, man begins perfect, and then ' falls ' into corruption, and grows worse. This is shallow talking. For, on the one hand, true science recognises that there is such a thing as degradation and deterioration among men; it traces out its results in the destruction of great empires and splendid civilisations, and finds it also among savages who have gone backwards instead of forwards. On the other hand, religion, where it knows its own business, never thinks of affirming that GOD made man perfect to start with. The Book of Genesis suggests no such idea. When the human body was fitted to be the dwelling-place of spirit, man, as a spiritual being, began his career; he was quite imperfect; he had everything to learn; he was simple as a child—'barbarous,' if you like. But he was not necessarily sinful. He need not have rebelled against GOD and the laws of his own nature. Had he retained his innocence, we cannot doubt that the history of human development would have been more rapid, more glorious— ah, how much more rapid and glorious!—than, in fact, it has been; for, in fact, it has been at every stage tainted by sin. The first sin is described in the third chapter of Genesis. That chapter, like its surroundings, is probably rather allegory than history. But it is inspired to teach us the deepest lessons of life. It is inspired to teach us the true character of sin. Sin is not human nature. It is the violation of the law of human nature. It is lawlessness. It is man refusing GOD and wanting to be a GOD to himself, and so failing under trial and putting his nature out of joint. This is always and everywhere the nature of sin. Original sin is the result of actual sins. Actual sins are always acts of will by which men reject GOD, try to be independent of GOD, and so violate the law of their nature. Sin is lawlessness.

JESUS CHRIST came to perfect human nature, but He came also to redeem it. He came to deal with human nature as *sinful*. He came both to purge it from the guilt and taint of past sins, and also so to restore and convert the wills of men that they might be free from the commission of actual sins in the future.

How is it, then, that JESUS CHRIST is our Redeemer?

1. Because He is the Second Adam. Born of a Virgin, He has a perfect manhood and a new manhood. In Him is a fresh creation of GOD, free from the baneful inheritance of past sins. He is the perfect man, both perfectly developed and flawlessly pure from taint or stain.

2. Because, as perfect man, He sets the perfect pattern of human life, and summons all men to conform to it. He sets the pattern of what human life, free from sin, is capable of being—the pattern of purity, and love, and devotion; and He summons all men to be as He is—to follow His example, to obey His commands.

But, as a true physician, He gauges the depth of the malady under which human nature suffers. He knows that the true pattern of life will stimulate in men the desire to resemble it. But He knows also that they cannot be as He is without a radical change. ' Except a man be born again he cannot see the kingdom of GOD.' ' Except ye be converted ye cannot enter into the kingdom of heaven.' But what is this conversion and new birth? How is it possible? How is it that ' the Lamb of GOD ' takes away the sin of the world ?

3. Because He makes a perfect expiation for all the sins which men have committed, and sets flowing a fountain of spiritual renewal, of new life, to deliver them for the future from the power of sin. But the meaning of these phrases will serve us for consideration in the chapters that follow.

Meanwhile, I would summon all social reformers, all persons who desire to improve human life, to see to it that they learn the lesson of the one Great Physician, the one true Redeemer of man. Education and sanitary reform and political change may do much for human life, but they will never remove the fundamental evil. That fundamental evil is sin. There is no removing of sin but by ' the new birth.' There is no one who can give ' the new birth ' but He who first gave birth to man and to all things —the Word and SON of GOD. The only true Redeemer is the Creator also, who for us men, and for our salvation, was incarnate and was made man.

Look at Him at the grave of Lazarus. ' Take ye away the stone,' He says.* There are many stones which lie on the graves of dead humanity, and prevent the free access of the life-giving Word. There are social burdens and political evils ; there are bad dwellings and bad drains; there is ignorance and hopelessness. ' Take ye away the stones.' But when ye have done it the dead men will not live. The sick men will not be whole. These are necessary reforms, but they are not the new life. JESUS only is the Resurrection and the Life. He only can say to the dead soul, ' Lazarus, come forth.'

* St. John xi. 39.

THE ATONEMENT

'Out of the bosom of eternal bliss
  In which He reignèd with His glorious Sire,
He down descended like a most demiss*
    And abject thrall, in flesh's frail attire,
  That He for him might pay sin's deadly hire,
    And him restore unto the happy state,
    In which he stood before his hapless fate.

'And look at last how of most wretched wights†
    He taken was, betrayed, and false accused;
  How with most scornful taunts, and fell despite
    He was reviled, disgraced, and foul abused:
  How scourged, how crowned, how buffeted, how bruised;
    And lastly how 'twixt robbers crucified,
    With bitter wounds through hands and feet and side.'

OUR LORD'S work for us falls under three distinct heads
—Example, Atonement, Renewal. Of these, the first two
express what He did *for us*, the last what He does *in us*.
But we are concerned in this chapter only with what He
did *for* us, or in our stead, without any co-operation of
ours; and, indeed, with only a part of this—with His work
of atonement, or propitiation of GOD.

JESUS CHRIST our LORD offered to GOD the FATHER,
especially by His death upon the cross, a sacrifice of
atonement or propitiation, by the merits of which alone
we sinful men can be accepted in spite of our unworthi-
ness, and our sins can be forgiven.

People have made many objections to this article of the

* *I.e.*, submissive.   † *I.e.*, folk.

Christian Creed, and, indeed, it has often been taught in such a way as to justify these objections : chiefly because CHRIST'S work *for us* has been separated from His work *in us*. But it is not my business now to deal directly with objections. My business now is to try and present the truth to you positively and simply, and to commend it to your consciences without any notice of objections made to it. And, indeed, the best way to combat objections is to teach the truth in such a way as not to occasion the objections. And I must say this also : If this truth has been much objected to, it has shown at least as much attractive power. It has appealed everywhere to the heart of sinners. Christians all over the world—conscious, as all men but the very careless must be, of sins against GOD—have found it fit in with their innermost wants. Thus, there has been no more popular doctrine than this, that ' if any man sin, we have an Advocate with the FATHER, JESUS CHRIST the righteous : and He is the propitiation for our sins.' Even among Pagans their ignorant and often horrible sacrifices have been only the attempt of yearning, but untaught, human hearts to find the best substitute they could for the great unknown truth of the Perfect Sacrifice after which they were feeling.

And I am sure we may take it for granted that a doctrine which has met so universal a human need, and found so universal a response in human consciences, must be in substance true.

A sacrifice of atonement, a great act of reparation to GOD ! Surely, if sin is not mere ignorance or weakness or folly, but is an offence against GOD our FATHER, with whom we were created to have fellowship, such an act of reparation must have been somehow necessary. A wise and good father knows that he cannot, for his son's own sake, forgive him when he has done wrong, unless he shows signs of sorrow, and any sign of sorrow must be a making amends in whatever way is possible. If a son has outraged his home by drunkenness or violence, the father would fail in his duty as a father if he were to behave to his son as if nothing had happened, and receive him into his confidence again before he had both felt and shown a sorrow for the outrage he had committed; and such sorrow must bring with it a readiness, even a desire, to suffer punishment or to make reparation for what has been done. Merely to pass over and ignore the offence would have this fatal result: the son would grow to believe that his offence was, after all, very natural sort of conduct, and that it did not much matter. He would lose his conscience of right and wrong.

GOD our FATHER for a long time 'passed over'* the sins of the nations of old. 'He suffered all nations to walk in their own ways.' These were the times of ignorance that GOD 'winked at.'† Through all these periods He gave no signs, because, in His wise providence, He left men everywhere to find out for themselves, by slow experience, what a miserable thing a sinful life is—a life alienated from GOD, even though it possess all the resources of intellect and civilisation. Then man's necessity became GOD's opportunity. GOD revealed Himself to mankind in JESUS CHRIST. He came forth to show man again his true destiny. He advanced with His free offer of pardon and fellowship with Himself. But this free offer of generosity on GOD's part must have been accompanied by some act on man's part which should show that he recognised the wickedness of sin, that he desired to make amends for it, that he acknowledged and respected the holiness of GOD and the justice of His punishments of sin. And for this moral necessity GOD Himself—the SON of GOD—by His becoming man, makes provision. This is the reason of CHRIST's atoning act.

CHRIST is not only the Revealer of GOD: He is also the Son of Man—the representative man. So as man He recognises the Divine holiness. He offers to GOD the

* Rom. iii. 25 (R.V.).   † Acts xvii. 30, xiv. 16.

sacrifice of a true and strict obedience; and when this obedience involved the sacrifice of His life, He did not shrink even from the shedding of His blood. He offered to GOD the sacrifice of an obedience unto death, even the death of the cross.

More than this, it is the ordinance of GOD that sin brings evil consequence, not on the sinner only, but on the family, the tribe, the race to which he belongs. This is one way in which GOD had always been teaching men that they are one body, one family, and that they cannot separate themselves from their fellow-men. Selfishness in men had led them to try and escape from this law, and to have as small a share as they might in the sad burden which human wickedness has laid upon our race. But our LORD did not try to escape from the law. He ' hid not Himself from His own flesh.' He entered into the common lot of man. He let Himself feel all the terrible burden. When human sin closed in upon Him in its blindness and its selfishness—the sins of Jews and Gentiles, rulers and common people—when they rejected Him and maltreated Him and crucified Him, He accepted the awful burden which human sin thus laid upon His shoulders. He accepted it as what the Holy FATHER willed Him to bear for man's sake—the cup which He willed Him to drink. He offered before the face of the FATHER the perfect sacrifice—not only of personal obedience, but also of the willingness to bear all the awful consequences of human sin.

This is the acceptable sacrifice—the sacrifice offered in the name of all humanity by the pattern Man: the flawless, spotless sacrifice of a perfect will, a perfect obedience, a patient endurance of other men's sins, showing itself in the willing shedding even to the last drop of His human blood. Upon this human offering, made by His own SON in our manhood, the FATHER looks down. All over the world He had beheld weakness and wilfulness and pollution and selfishness. Now for the first and only time

He beholds a human life and death, perfectly acceptable, rendered to Himself as a voluntary offering. Now for the first time is He perfectly 'well pleased' in the spectacle of man. Now for the first time is adequate and perfect reparation made in man's name to His offended majesty and love. Now does He behold a propitiation which will enable Him without serious moral misunderstanding to bestow upon the whole human race a free forgiveness, available for everyone who will come and throw himself on the love of the FATHER simply in faith in JESUS CHRIST the SON.

This is a great subject, and I have space to say very little. I must be content to leave my readers with these thoughts:

1. The reason for our LORD's Atonement appears to have lain in the necessity that some great central act of reparation should be made in man's name to the offended majesty and righteousness of GOD, so that, as it were, GOD might be free to offer him forgiveness without the conscience of mankind becoming dulled to the true hatefulness of sin.

2. CHRIST, who offers the great sacrifice of Atonement, offers it as the representative Man. But He who offers it is also in our manhood very GOD. So that GOD Himself supplies the sacrifice which the moral situation requires—itself a free gift of His love.

3. It is available for every man who will accept it in faith. This act of faith is in one way the easiest of all acts. It is the mere recognition of our need, and the acceptance of a Divine gift free and unmerited. But this act of faith by which a man accepts his forgiveness is itself the pledge that he takes CHRIST for his Master, and will grow into union with that obedience, and patience, and zeal for GOD's honour in which He offered the sacrifice. The offer of pardon and acceptance, for the merit of CHRIST's sacrifice, to everyone who has faith in JESUS, is of all offers the most liberal,

But yet this simple faith is itself the seed of all true righteousness.

But this is a line of thought that we must follow further in another chapter.

4. It is commonly supposed that CHRIST suffered for us in order that we might be let off suffering. May I ask my readers to notice that this way of speaking cannot be justified from the New Testament ? CHRIST is there represented as suffering in order (1) that we might be forgiven and reconciled to GOD; (2) that we might share CHRIST'S life and have fellowship with His sufferings. There is no passage in the New Testament which naturally suggests that there is any sort of suffering which CHRIST suffered which we are not also called to suffer in our degree.* If there is such a passage, I wish one of my readers would show it to me.

5. I spoke above of the ' times of ignorance,' the ' times which GOD winked at,' as lying in the past, and being brought to a close by CHRIST'S coming in the flesh. So the New Testament speaks of them. So, in fact, they were brought to an end for all Greeks or Romans who came within hearing of the Gospel. But they still went on for other nations. They went on for hundreds of years for our Saxon forefathers. They are continuing still— these times of ignorance—for Chinese and Japanese and Hindus, who have either not heard the Gospel or not really felt it in its power. But for them, too, as for Greeks and Romans and Teutons and Celts, there will come the moment of Divine opportunity. And when it arrives the provision is ready. For since CHRIST appeared and His witness has been borne in the world, wherever the message of the Gospel has gone it has contained in the preaching of the atoning sacrifice the remedy for all careless thoughts about sin.

---

* See 1 St. Pet. ii. 21-24, iv. 1. This is the general sense of the New Testament.

Here, then, is the blessed truth for us. GOD hates sin. But 'if we confess our sins, He is faithful and righteous to forgive us our sins.' For 'if any man sin, we have an Advocate with the FATHER, JESUS CHRIST the righteous: and He is the propitiation for our sins; and not for ours only, but also for the whole world.'*

* 1 St. John i. 9, ii. 1, 2.

' O Thou, who keep'st the key of love,
  Open Thy fount, eternal Dove,
    And overflow this heart of mine,
  Enlarging as it fills with Thee,
  Till in one blaze of charity
Care and remorse are lost, like motes in light divine :

' Till, as each moment wafts us higher,
  By every gush of pure desire,
    And high-breathed hope of joys above,
  By every secret sigh we heave,
  Whole years of folly we outlive
In His unerring sight, who measures life by love.'

In my last paper I was considering how it is that GOD the FATHER forgives us our past sins by the merits of CHRIST'S perfect sacrifice. Much as there is in this mystery of Atonement which we cannot fathom, the offer of GOD there made to us is practically plain. If a man come before GOD in penitence for his sins, and with faith in JESUS, GOD will forgive him his sins—that is, will not impute them to him, or will reckon them as if they did not exist.

But does GOD, then, ' make believe'? The sins are real acts of the man; they still, though he repent of them, belong to his character. How can GOD, who is the True, reckon them as if they were not ? I answer, Because GOD *sees us and deals with us, not as we are, but as we are becoming.* The truest judgment of any person or thing is one which takes into account what he or it is to become. Why do I buy a cutting of a valuable plant, though it be but a little bit of stick, at a high price ? Because of what it is

going to become. So it is that GOD reckons the penitent
and believing sinner at what he is going to become. At
present he is not righteous, but his penitence and faith are
the seed of a full righteousness yet to grow in him.

But perhaps, you say, it will not grow. What then?
Ah yes, alas! Perhaps it will not grow. Perhaps the
man will fall away. Then all the forgivenesses which
GOD has given him on his repentances for his repeated
sins will fall away, too. Till the last great acquittal at
the day of death and judgment, all GOD's absolutions are
provisional, not final. So our LORD teaches us in the
parable of the unthankful servant.* His master, you
remember, forgave him his heavy debts when he could
not pay them. But he went out and at once behaved
hardly and unforgivingly towards a fellow-servant who
owed a trifle to him. When this was known, he was
summoned back before his master, and *found all his own
debts back upon him.* 'He was delivered to the tormentors
till he should pay all that was due. So likewise,' our
LORD adds, 'shall My Heavenly FATHER do also unto
you if ye' behave not in a manner becoming those who
have had much forgiven them. GOD's forgivenesses of us
are not yet final or irrevocable.

Now we can see how the matter stands a little more
clearly. At the last great acquittal GOD will forgive us
our sins finally and for ever, because they no longer belong
to our changed characters, as Saul the persecutor's sins
no longer belong to Paul the Apostle. We shall have
grown out of them. But meanwhile, at the very beginning of our course—and again and again upon the road—
at the first movement of repentance and faith, GOD forgives
us what we have done amiss; He reckons our sins as if
they did not exist, and setting us thus rid of their burden
and their bondage, leaves us free to run the way of His
commandments.

GOD is never tired of forgiving us in this way. He is

* St. Matt. xviii. 23.

never tired of our fresh beginnings. Indeed, there is no real failure in religion except to give up trying; to refuse any more to be sorry for the past, and to make a fresh start.

But the end of all GOD's dealings with us is that we should be made at last actually righteous; that we should be rid, not merely of the guilt of sin, but of its power. Everything in religion is, indeed, a means of this one end —that we may be brought back into actual living union with GOD; and this, of course, means actual likeness to GOD.

How is this to be? By faith, you say. Yes. 'Thy faith shall make thee whole.' But what is faith? It is, as it were, the open hand, or open mouth, of the human soul. It welcomes GOD's promise; it expects His gift. What is the gift which it expects and welcomes? It is the HOLY SPIRIT, the LORD and Giver of life. When JESUS was on earth healing men's bodies, it was their faith which made them whole. But how? Because their faith set free to work upon them the healing ' virtue ' or power which went out of CHRIST. That healing virtue or power was the virtue and power of the HOLY GHOST in His sacred humanity. And still JESUS makes us whole, in soul and spirit first of all, by bestowing upon us out of His sacred manhood the gift of the HOLY SPIRIT.

GOD the HOLY SPIRIT is, as you know, the Third Person of the Blessed TRINITY. He has always been at work in the world, and especially as the giver of life. All life in nature, in plants, in animals, in man, is His presence and gift. So the human life of JESUS, His human holiness, the strength in which He overcame Satan and wrought miracles, was His gift. The FATHER anointed JESUS of Nazareth with the HOLY GHOST without measure. And when He rose to the right hand of the FATHER, this, and nothing but this, was the gift of JESUS to His fellow-men—the gift of the HOLY SPIRIT. He is the 'other Comforter,' or ' Helper,' who was to take the place of

JESUS when He went.* Ah! but that will not half express the truth. '*I* will not leave you comfortless,' our LORD continued; '*I* will come unto you.'† '*We* (My FATHER and I) will come and make *Our* abode with you.'‡ For the three Persons of the Blessed TRINITY are not separable individuals. They are one personal GOD. So where One is All are. The HOLY SPIRIT does not come alone; He in His coming brings with Him the SON and the FATHER. This, then, is the great truth of Pentecost. GOD the HOLY GHOST came down out of the sacred and glorified manhood of our LORD, bringing with Him, not merely the presence of the FATHER, but the presence also of the Man CHRIST JESUS, the SON incarnate. That is it: the HOLY SPIRIT came to dwell in the Church, and in every member of the Church, and He brings with Him all the power, the excellence, of the glorified manhood of CHRIST. The SPIRIT is the Life-giver. But the life which He gives—the life into which He implants us, the life with which He nourishes and strengthens us—is the life of the glorified JESUS. The HOLY SPIRIT dwells in us, and for that very reason it is ' CHRIST in us,' the hope of glory.

CHRIST in us! What a mistake Christians make when they think of GOD, of CHRIST, the SON of GOD, as far off! He is our life; He is within us.

' Speak to Him, thou, for He hears, and Spirit with spirit can meet;
Closer is He than breathing, and nearer than hands and feet.'

This is it which makes it so plain how CHRIST'S example is of use to us. People often argue that, if CHRIST was sinless, His example can be of no use to us. Perhaps not, if He were only example. Perhaps His life would strike us, so pure is it, with nothing else than despair. It would be too high for us to follow. But, in fact, His example, and His atoning sacrifice also, are only parts of His work. He who acts *for us* as our representative also acts *in us* as our new life. That very JESUS whose life we

* St. John xiv. 16.   † *Ibid.*, xiv. 18.   ‡ *Ibid.*, xiv. 23.

read of in the Gospels, that very JESUS who conquered
Satan so that he fled away to hide his head in hell, is both
before our eyes as our example, and also in us, by His
SPIRIT, as our new life. It is CHRIST in us, who forms us
by His SPIRIT inwardly upon the model of the pattern
which He showed us outwardly.

Who shall despair, then ? However often we fall, we
have GOD ready to forgive us for CHRIST's sake. And however weak we are, we have CHRIST in us, by His SPIRIT,
ready to strengthen us and make us like Him. Never let
us despair, then. Let us hold on to JESUS, our Example,
our Sacrifice, our New Life. There is no failure except in
ceasing to try ; we can never be lost except by deliberately
abandoning GOD.

THE BIBLE IN THE CHURCH

' Here the same Fountain poureth forth
  Water, wine, milk, oil, honey; and the worth
    Of all transcendent, infinite
  In excellence, and to each appetite
    In fitness answerable ; so
  That none need hence unsatisfièd go,
  Whose stomach serves him unto anything
  That health, strength, comfort, or content can bring.'

' GRACE and truth came by JESUS CHRIST.'

These are the two great spiritual goods for men. Man needs light for his intelligence, and strength for his will—guidance for his mind, and power in his life. Both of these JESUS gives him. But in this paper we are only concerned with one of them—the light, the guidance for the mind, the truth.

Truth came by JESUS CHRIST. He declared Himself to be the Truth. And as you read the Gospels you see He cared for nothing more than to impart it. When the world in general would not receive it, He chose those who would—His twelve Apostles ; and He gave all His attention to teaching them, not about science, or history, or politics, but about GOD and man. He taught them the truth about GOD, His character, His being; about the FATHER; about Himself, the SON; about the HOLY GHOST, whom He was to send. He taught them the truth about themselves, about human nature—its capacity, its responsibility, its destiny, its sin. He taught them about the kingdom of GOD which was to come, and the Church which was to represent the kingdom, and to prepare for it. This truth He did not write down. JESUS CHRIST left nothing written behind him. He left His legacy of truth engrained into the memories of a small body of men by years of intercourse with Himself—years in which He was training, teaching, rebuking, helping, encouraging them. When He left the world, He left these men to be witnesses of the truth which he had come to reveal; and He first before His death promised, and at Pentecost gave, them a special gift of the HOLY GHOST to assist and guarantee what they had gained by natural training. 'The Comforter,' He said, 'which is the HOLY GHOST, whom the FATHER will send in My name, He shall teach you all things, and bring all things to your remembrance, whatsoever I have said unto you.'*

The Apostles, then, were left to bear witness to the truth as it is in JESUS, for all generations of men.

And how did they bear witness? 'By writing the books of the New Testament,' I hear someone reply. Yes, but not first of all. The books of the New Testament were not written to give men their first knowledge of JESUS. They were written for men who already possessed it, who had already been instructed. Will my readers take the pains to look out the following texts in the New Testament—in the Revised Version if they have got it (as they should have); if not, in the Old Version: St. Luke i. 4; 1 Cor. xi. 2, 23, xv. 1-4; Gal. i. 8; Heb. v. 11, vi. 3; 2 St. Pet. i. 12; 1 St. John ii. 21; St. Jas. i. 19 (R.V.); Jude 3. These texts will make it plain to anyone that the books of the New Testament were written for men and women who had already been taught 'the tradition,' 'the faith once for all delivered,' 'the first principles' of the Christian religion. The books of the New Testament were intended to remind them of what they already knew, to recall it to their minds, and to build them up in further knowledge of it, 'that they might know the certainty of those things in which they had already been (orally)

* St. John xiv. 26.

instructed.' That is to say, oral teaching or catechising
—the substance of which is called 'the tradition '—was
the first means of imparting Christian truth. In the Acts
we learn how the first Christians were orally instructed in
' the Apostles' doctrine.'*

A further study of the New Testament will convince
anyone that it is not the sort of book which is calculated
to give people their first ideas of religion. All that people
need to be taught first is assumed as already known ; all,
for example, that is contained in our Creed and Catechism.
This is not taught, but referred to. The Name—that is,
the revelation—of FATHER, SON, and HOLY GHOST ; the
outlines of the life of our LORD ; the moral duties of
religion ; the Church ; the Sacraments and their value ;
the judgment to come—all this (as the texts above referred
to will make plain) are presupposed as things already
known.

Not only is this the case, but we can see why it should
be. Our LORD intended that men should learn, not from
books, but from persons ; all His methods show us this.
This is why He taught His Apostles to be witnesses,
instead of writing Himself or teaching them to write.
And, further, He did not mean men to learn from mere
individual teachers, however much inspired. He formed
a Church, or organised body, and He left to the Church
the duty of being witness to the truth till He should come
again. It is the Church which, as St. Paul says, is ' the
pillar and ground of the truth.' †

Thus, the Apostles, as we learn in the Acts, founded a
branch of the Church in every place, and ordained officers
to keep it in order and to hand on the truth. And when
the Apostles were looking forward to their own deaths,
they contemplated the truth being carried on by ' faithful
men,' who should succeed them in their teaching office.
' The things which thou hast heard from me among many
witnesses,' wrote St. Paul to the Apostolic legate or

* Acts ii. 42.   † 1 Tim. iii. 15.

bishop, Timothy, 'the same commit thou to faithful men, who shall be able to teach others also.'* This is what is called the 'Apostolic succession,' which was intended to secure in every church a due succession all down the ages of authorised and instructed teachers of 'the Apostolic doctrine.'

So far the truth rests upon *tradition*. But, then, every-one knows that 'tradition' by itself is not a very safe foundation for truth. After it has been handed down through two or three generations, certain things are sure to have come about. The statement of truth has become hardened and formal; it lacks vital inspiration; it has become corrupted by the admixture of alien elements; it has become one-sided through those points which are most popular in one generation having special stress laid on them to the neglect of others. In other words, mere tradition tends to become hard, corrupt, and one-sided. It wants continually rectifying, continually recalling to its original type, supposing the type a good and complete one, which we know the 'Apostles' doctrine' was. How is this to be secured? Here comes in the function of the Bible? The Apostles, and the Apostolic men who com-panied with them, did not only teach: they also, as occasion served, wrote the books of the New Testament, which the Church collected into one book and added to the Old Testament Scriptures. Here we have, then, a continual court of appeal. The living Church must do the teaching in every generation, but the written Book must continually test and correct the teaching. The Church must teach, but the Bible must prove. ' *Do not believe what I say simply,*' says an old Church teacher and Bishop, Cyril of Jerusalem, in his catechetical lectures, ' *unless you find the proof of it in the Holy Scriptures.* Here is the true ideal—the Bishop or Church teaching; the Bible, continually in the hands of all Church people, keeping the teaching pure.

* 2 Tim. ii. 2.

Now, in my next chapter I hope to go on to show why the Bible, as an inspired Book, is qualified to fulfil the office of a continual court of appeal. In other words, I hope to write on *the Inspiration of Scripture*. But here I must be content with showing you thus, in outline, what is the place of the Bible, and especially of the New Testament, in the teaching Church. I must be content with having shown you that the truth which, as Christians, we value does not rest upon one foundation, but two: not on tradition only, but on tradition *and* Scripture; nor on two foundations only, but on three, for I must not forget the 'unction of the HOLY GHOST '—the personal illumination given to every Christian. Here are *three* supports, no one of which is sufficient by itself—the Bible, the Church, the individual mind and conscience.

> ' These are the three great chords of might ;
> And he whose ear is tuned aright
> Will hear no discord in the three,
> But the most perfect harmony.'

And now, if this is true, have we not reason to be thankful to the Church of England ? Whatever her faults, she, more than any branch of the Church Catholic, holds together Church authority, Bible authority, and individual conscience. The Church of Rome makes much of one; Protestantism makes much of the other two. But the Church of England, like the Church of primitive days, holds these together. She teaches us the tradition first of all, as it is given in the Creeds and the Catechism, and then she puts the open Bible into the hands of all of us, and bids us build ourselves up in the further knowledge of those things wherein we have been instructed; and by this further Biblical knowledge which she desires all her children to have she means that a continually purifying influence should be exercised in the current Church teaching, as ' men search the Scripture,' and see if the things taught them in sermon and Catechism are there indeed.

THE INSPIRATION OF SCRIPTURE

> ' It is the looking-glass of souls, wherein
>> All souls may see
>> Whether they be
> Still, as by nature they are, deformed with sin ;
>> Or in a better case
>> As new-adorned with grace.
>
> 'Tis the great magazine of spiritual arms,
>> Wherein doth lie
>> The artillery
> Of heaven, ready charged against all harms
>> That might come by the blows
>> Of our infernal foes.'

THE Bible, we have seen, is to be our continual standard of spiritual truth. We are continually to go back to it and ' search the Scriptures, whether the things ' we hear and read about GOD and man ' are so ' indeed. And the reason why we can use the Bible as a permanent standard of spiritual truth is because the writers of it are ' inspired ' men. Now we must consider a little more closely what this means. And we will begin with the Apostles.

The Apostles, we saw, were trained to be witnesses. And when you need to try and convince a doubter of the truth of the Christian religion, you should not argue with him about the *inspiration* of the writers of the Bible. All that you should try and prove to him is that the Apostles were credible and trustworthy witnesses of what they had seen and heard, and that their witness remains with us in the New Testament. But those who are already Christians will believe the Apostles to be witnesses, and something more.

No man can come to believe in JESUS without believing also in the SPIRIT whom JESUS sent to take His place in the Church. All that can attract men in good Christians, and draw them to believe in GOD, is the work of this HOLY SPIRIT. He inhabits and breathes His influence into (that is, *inspires*) all Christian people. But He does not inspire all Christian people equally. ' There are diversities of gifts.' And the highest gift of inspiration belonged to the Apostles. Thus, St. John* tells us that our LORD before His death gave them this promise: ' The HOLY GHOST, whom the FATHER will send in My name, He shall teach you all things, and bring all things to your remembrance, whatsoever I have said unto you.' Accordingly, St. John believed himself to be inspired. ' I was in the SPIRIT [that is, *inspired*] on the LORD's day,' he writes at the beginning of the Revelation,† and therefore he claims Divine authority for his message or prophecy.‡ So at the beginning of his Epistle he writes as one who has undoubted Divine authority to proclaim ' the message which we have heard from GOD and announce unto you.'§ Just in the same way St. Paul claims that what he preaches is a Divine revelation made personally by GOD to himself,‖ and for this reason he commends the Thessalonians because they received his message, ' not as the word of men, but, as it is in truth, the Word of God.'¶ At times, indeed, St. Paul gives what is only a private opinion of his own—as that celibacy is better than marriage for a Christian under circumstances of special strain, and in such a case he expressly says he has not Divine authority for what he says;** but this distinction which he here draws between his own opinion and the commandment of the LORD only gives us more confidence in his claim to Divine inspiration when he makes it.

The Apostles, then, claim to be personally inspired in

---

* St. John xiv. 26.   † Rev. i. 10.   ‡ *Ibid.*, xxii. 18, 19.
§ 1 St. John i. 1-5.   ‖ Gal. i. 11-16.
¶ 1 Thess. ii. 13.   ** 1 Cor. vii. 6, 12, 25.

accordance with our LORD'S promise, and therefore to be
authoritative or perfectly trustworthy teachers of the
Word of GOD. And the earliest Church, which knew
them personally in all their trials and tribulations, believed
them to be all that they claimed to be, and more; and all
down the Christian generations men have gone on putting
their claim to the test and finding it true. There is no
exact dogma *about* inspiration which we are required as
Churchmen to receive, but the reality of the inspiration of
the Apostles is an inherited belief of the Church, continually proved true in the consciences and intellects
of prayerful Christians.

Nor did the twelve Apostles stand alone; round about
them were men also inspired, ' prophets ' like Barnabas
and Apollos.* From one of such Apostolic men we have
the Epistle to the Hebrews, and from companions of the
Apostles we have the Gospel of St. Mark, the Gospel of
St. Luke, and the Acts. A tone of Apostolic authority
runs through the Epistle to the Hebrews, and respect was
paid to it as to an Apostolic book from the earliest days in
the Christian Church. It is, in fact, the fountain head of
all that the Church has believed about the High Priesthood
of our LORD. St. Luke in his preface to his Gospel† only
lays claim to accuracy and the fullest opportunity of the
best information. But he depends upon the inspired
testimony of the Apostles; and we cannot doubt that the
Church of all ages has been right in recognising that he
and the other Evangelists who only collected the best
material for their Gospel narratives, and who invented
nothing, yet were fitted for their work by a special gift
of the HOLY GHOST.

So far, then, about the inspiration of the New Testament. The belief in this inspiration was made easy at
starting by the fact that the first Christians already
believed in books written by inspired men—the books of
the Old Testament. ' Every Scripture inspired of God,'

---

* Acts xi. 24, xiii. 1 ; 1 Cor. iii. 4-6.   † St. Luke i. 1-4.

so St. Paul refers to the Old Testament.* And, indeed, our LORD's language about the Old Testament had put it beyond doubt for faithful Christians that the Old Testament was really inspired, and contained 'the Word of GOD.'†

In the Old Testament, as in the New, we find inspiration of different kinds and degrees. The highest kind is the inspiration of the prophets, who claim in the most direct way to speak the Word of the LORD. They were very different men one from another, and were all of them, in their different ways, fallible men; but they proclaimed a great deal of truth about GOD—His holiness: His claims on men: His dealings with nations: His purpose for His chosen people: His intention to bring salvation to the Jews and to mankind through a Messiah. And now that the centuries have rolled by, we can be sure that their claims to inspiration, verified and certified by our LORD, by the Apostles and the Church, is a true one. 'The spirit of prophecy' in them was 'the testimony of JESUS.' 'No prophecy ever came by the will of man; but men spake from GOD, being moved by the HOLY GHOST.'‡

Nor can we study the Psalms, and make them the language of our own prayer and praise, without recognising that—in spite of imperfections such as belong to the Old Testament time, like the personal imprecations upon enemies which occur in some of the Psalms§—the spiritual life depicted there, in its height and depth and breadth, is the work of none other than the HOLY SPIRIT of GOD. No testimony to this can be stronger than that which holy souls in all ages have made and are making to the Psalms.

* 2 Tim. iii. 16.

† See especially St. Luke xxiv. 26, 27, 44, 45; St. Mark vii. 13; St. Matt. v. 18.

‡ 2 St. Pet. i. 21.

§ Even these imprecations, though they fall short of the Christian spirit (St. Luke ix. 54-56), contain important truth about Divine judgments (St. Luke xviii. 7; Rev. vi. 10; Acts i. 20).

In a somewhat different way we recognise Divine in-struction in the Old Testament histories. The Book of Genesis opens not with idle fables about how the world came into being—like the Pagan mythologies—but with an account which, in all spiritual matters is for ever true : that the one GOD made all things ; that all things are in their true nature and use very good ; that the real misery of man, his 'fall,' comes not from Nature, but from his own disobedience ; and that even in his fallen state man is still not left without the providence of the good GOD, slowly working out His righteous and loving purpose. The truth of the revelation is not affected by our believing that the narrative in which it is conveyed is allegorical and not literal history. The 'history' of the Old Testa-ment passes through all the same stages of literary method as any other history. There is allegory, and tradition, and popular song, and dry chronicle, and moral lesson ; but through them all there runs the inspiration of GOD, so that the record is throughout made to serve a right purpose, and to display, not man's vanity, but GOD's providence. And in books like Ecclesiastes or Proverbs or Job we see how the SPIRIT of GOD can brood over and direct the early thoughts of men as they meditate upon the mysteries of Nature and human existence. So it is that in ' many parts' and ' many manners' GOD spake of old times unto our fathers. He who spoke was GOD's SPIRIT. Thus, the Old Testament contains the Word of GOD. And this Word or message of GOD came to its highest and fullest and deepest expression in the revelation of the CHRIST and in the inspiration of His Apostles.

This is the common belief of Christians of all ages. The exact nature of the inspiration of the Old and New Testament writers men have often tried to define, but never very successfully. Certainly no one has a right to impose on his fellows any particular belief about inspira-tion, its nature and its limits. But what has been said above describes its general character ; and this, at least, has been always believed about it. And we in our day can take this Christian belief on trust, and put it to the proof for ourselves; and in all that concerns spiritual things—the things (as they are called) of faith and morals—we shall find that this belief is justified to our own consciences and hearts. We shall not try and pick a religion out of the Bible for ourselves—the Bible was not meant to be so used—but taught, as we are, the Church's common creed, we shall, by continual use of the Bible, build ourselves up in the knowledge of our most holy faith.

THE CHURCH THE HOUSEHOLD OF GRACE

'Where is that fire which once descended
On the Apostles? Thou didst then
Keep open house, richly attended,
Feasting all comers by twelve chosen men.
Such glorious gifts Thou didst bestow
That the earth did like a heaven appear ;
The stars were coming down to know
If they might mend their wages and serve here.
*   *   *   *   *
LORD, though we change, Thou art the same ;
The same sweet GOD of love and light
Restore this day,* for Thy good Name,
Unto His ancient and miraculous right.'

IT has already appeared that GOD'S gift of saving truth,
offered to men in JESUS CHRIST, is offered them, not singly,
but as members of the society or Church to which the
truth is committed to be handed down. This is according
to our nature. The gifts of civilisation, the gifts of knowledge and wealth and personal liberty, have come to men
only as members of a race or state or nation. So the gifts
of religion, the gifts of spiritual truth and grace, are
promised to men only in the great Christian society, the
Catholic Church.

That this is the case with Christian truth has already
appeared. But it is no less the case with the gifts of
grace given us in JESUS CHRIST. It is as the rich de-
pository of this grace that the Church is called 'the
household of GOD.'

A household—a home. These are words that carry

* Whit-Sunday.

a plain meaning to every heart and head. At home one is comforted, one moves at ease, one is provided for, and one's ordinary wants are satisfied. There, too (if it is to be worthy of the name), there must be peace, order, and discipline. Thus, when the Church is called the 'household of GOD' the word carries with it all these thoughts about home. In the Church men are to be taken out of their solitude, and provided for as in a family, and feel about them the warmth of human fellowship.

Ah yes! human fellowship. We must take care that in every one of our churches, as far as may be, the family feeling is kept up. Members of a church ought to feel themselves taken out of their solitude. By whatever means it is to be brought about, churches must be true to the Divine intention, 'He setteth the solitary in families.'*

But human fellowship is not all. St. John writes his Epistle that his readers 'may have fellowship with us '— that is, human fellowship—but he does not stop there. 'Truly,' he adds, 'our fellowship is with the FATHER and with His SON JESUS CHRIST.'† Here we get to the root of the matter. The Church is the household of GOD, because in it, through human fellowship, GOD the HOLY GHOST conveys to us all the gifts of CHRIST—that is, the gifts of the life of GOD Himself.

These gifts of CHRIST are 'the Bread of Life'; and, as is proper in a household, the bread is given to us at due times and seasons. In the Church is a rich provision for human needs, a rich provision accompanying our life from the cradle to the grave, offering to us at each stage of life's day our 'portion of meat in due season.'‡

The beginning of life is to be born, and the beginning of our Christian life is to be 'born again of water and the SPIRIT.' In the case of those whose parents are members of the Christian family, or for whom the Church undertakes to be in place of parents, the birth and the new birth

* Ps. lxviii. 6.   † 1 St. John i. 3.   ‡ St. Luke xii. 42.

come close together. While still infants they are made 'members of CHRIST' in Baptism, so that the life of CHRIST may accompany and consecrate the very beginnings of feeling and intelligence.

Then as the child grows on its independent life begins. And as it passes into boyhood or girlhood this new stage of life is met with a new gift. In Confirmation the growing soul is filled with the gift of the HOLY GHOST, and thus given its proper share in the priesthood and kingship of JESUS CHRIST, its LORD. And after that there is continual nourishment. As the life of the body is sustained with regular meals, so the life of the soul is regularly nourished with the body and blood of JESUS—that is, the very essence of His person, human and Divine, in Holy Communion. These are the highest gifts of the SPIRIT, but they are not all.

Sin may have wrought its destruction in the soul, and the Christian may have fallen away from the Divine fellowship. It may have become dead again in trespasses and sins. To meet so grievous a disaster there is the gift of restoration, 'the plank after shipwreck.' The sinner confesses his sin, he submits himself to the judgment of the Church in what the Prayer-Book calls 'Penance,'* and, like a prodigal restored to his family, he is welcomed back by absolution into the 'holy fellowship.' Or the time has come when the grown life of a man is to be completed by union with a woman in one flesh. Again the Church is present to sanctify the union and bless the foundation of a new family in Holy Matrimony. Once again, this or that man is called to take upon himself the high office of a 'steward' in the Divine household, to administer to others the Bread of Life by which he himself lives. Here again the Church, in its holy Ordination, imparts to him the authority and power for this new ministry. Once more, when grave sickness is upon any Christian, the Church, as in Apostolic days, is present with the remedial anointing

* See Article XXXIII. and Commination Service.

of the Holy Oil,* or, at least, where this rite has been abandoned, with other holy ministries; and if the sickness be unto death, she stands full of the hope of immortality, to usher the soul into the unseen world.

Verily, the Church is the household of GOD, the home of our spiritual life, because at each crisis and turning she is by our side with a blessed provision for our needs as they occur; and the provision in each case is a great spiritual gift conveyed through the simplest possible forms, intelligible and acceptable to every head and every heart. For GOD is a GOD of simplicity and power, and He gives, therefore, the highest gifts through the simplest channels. Our nature also is made up of body and soul, and the gifts for the soul are therefore given us through bodily and visible channels.

There are many people who have found difficulties in the sacramental system; but, after all, if this is a true general account of the Sacraments and ministries of grace, is it not intelligible to us all? Does it not appeal to what is best and simplest in us?

* St. Jas. v. 14.

FAITH AND GRACE

' If bliss had lien in art or strength,
  None but the wise and strong had gained it ;
Where now by faith all arms are of a length,
  One size doth all conditions fit.
A peasant may believe as much
  As a great clerk, and reach the highest stature ;
Thus dost Thou make proud knowledge bend and crouch,
  While grace fills up uneven nature.'

I SHALL have something more to say in other chapters
about some of the Sacraments, but I want to stop at this
point and try to explain a difficulty with which we are
often met. Again and again people reply to the sort of
teaching about the Sacraments which I tried to give in
the last chapter : ' But I cannot attribute so much im-
portance to ceremonies. According to the Gospels and
St. Paul, it is by faith we are saved.' And then, by way
of proving that the belief of the Church in the Sacraments is mistaken, they point to the multitude of baptized
people who are living wicked or careless lives, and ask
triumphantly whether it is possible to believe that those
people are the possessors of the new birth of the HOLY
SPIRIT. In view of such a very common objection, I want
to make it quite plain that the Christian Church has
never taught that either Baptism or any of the Sacraments
can make men good by merely being administered to them.
Besides Sacraments, faith and conversion are ' necessary
to salvation ' in the case of each separate individual ; and
it is only by an extraordinary mistake that Sacraments on
the one side, and faith and conversion on the other, have
ever been torn asunder in Christian preaching.

Suppose two savages looking on at a musician playing a violin. They think they would like to make that noise themselves. So they set upon the performer, and one of them gets hold of the bow and makes off with it, and proceeds to scrape it violently upon all sorts of pieces of wood, and is much disappointed because he cannot induce the horsehair to make any sound at all. And the other gets hold of the fiddle with the catgut strings and carries that into a corner, and, after scraping it diligently with a bit of stick, throws it down disgusted because he, too, fails to produce any satisfactory noise. You would watch the proceedings of those two savages with some amusement, but in fact their conduct would not be a bad illustration of what one-sided believers in faith and one-sided believers in Sacraments have been constantly doing. They have each of them been running off with half a truth, or trying to produce by means of one half of a piece of spiritual machinery a result which can only be truly produced by both halves in combination.

The 'Bread of Life' given us in the 'household of GOD' is like common bread in this, that it cannot nourish or do any good to us unless it be eaten with some appetite and digested into our system. Food given from without, and appetite and digestion supplied from within, are alike necessary to our physical life. So in the same way the Sacraments actually convey to us the food of our souls as a gift given from without; but they do us no good unless there be a spirit in us awake to what is being given, welcoming the gift and ready to 'assimilate' or digest it into our spiritual system.

Think of our LORD's healings. There was a 'virtue' or 'power' which went out from His sacred humanity, and which made men whole. But it only made men whole if they had faith to desire it and to accept it. Thus, it is said of our LORD at one place, that He 'could do there no mighty work . . . because of their unbelief.'*

* St. Mark vi. 5, 6; St. Matt. xiii. 58.

At other times He said to those who 'had faith to be
healed,' 'Thy faith hath saved thee,' 'According to
thy faith be it unto thee'—not because faith could heal
by itself, but because faith gave men the power to desire
and appropriate the gifts of CHRIST. On another occasion,
when multitudes 'thronged Him,' He said of one woman
that she 'touched Him,' because He 'perceived that
virtue had gone out of Him'*—that is, out of a great
crowd one woman only had the faith necessary to draw
out upon herself the blessings which were there for all.
So the grace of Baptism or of Holy Communion is the
same for all : the gift in each case is what it is by CHRIST's
power and the power of His SPIRIT : in the case of Baptism
it is the sharing in the new life ; in the other case, the
body and blood of CHRIST. But though multitudes receive
the gifts, only some appropriate them by faith ; multitudes
'throng' CHRIST, but only a few 'touch' Him.

Now, surely, we can see why our LORD should have said
on the one hand, 'Except a man be born of water and
the SPIRIT, he cannot enter into the kingdom of GOD,'† and
'Except ye eat the flesh of the SON of GOD, and drink
His blood, ye have not life in yourselves;'‡ and on the
other hand, 'This is the work of GOD, that ye believe
on Him whom He hath sent,'§ and 'Except ye be
converted [or *turn*, which is the same as having the will to
believe in CHRIST] ye cannot enter into the kingdom of
heaven.'‖ Now we can understand why St. Paul should
sometimes speak so clearly of the Sacraments, calling
Baptism 'the laver of regeneration,' speaking of our being
'baptized into CHRIST,' administering Confirmation in
order to bestow the gift of the HOLY GHOST, speaking of
our communicating in the body and blood of CHRIST in
the Eucharist, reminding Timothy of the gift that was in
Him through the laying on of hands ;¶ and, on the other

* St. Mark v. 30-34.   † St. John iii. 5.   ‡ *Ibid.*, vi. 53.
§ *Ibid.*, vi. 29.   ‖ St. Matt. xviii. 3.
¶ Tit. iii. 5 ; Rom. vi. 3 ; Acts xix. 1-6 ; 1 Cor. x. 16, 17 ; 2 Tim. i. 6.

hand, should assert so confidently that nothing but faith 'justifies' us or commends us to GOD, and that we have ' access by faith into that grace wherein we stand.'*

Three times over St. Paul states the one necessity in the Christian religion, by contrast to the mere bodily distinction between Jew and Gentile, circumcision or uncircumcision. Once he says, ' Circumcision is nothing, and uncircumcision is nothing, but *a new creature* '—that is, the gift of ' grace.'† Next, ' Neither circumcision availeth anything, nor uncircumcision, but *faith working by love* ' —that is, operative faith.‡ Once more, ' Circumcision is nothing, and uncircumcision is nothing, but the *keeping of the commandments of GOD* '—that is, the actual obedience which is the one end and test alike of faith and of fellowship in the Sacraments.§ These three things are, in fact, but the one same spiritual life looked at from different points of view.

Now I hope we shall understand that faith and Sacraments are in no conflict the one with the other. You have no more got to choose between them, to take one *or* the other, than, when you want to play the fiddle, you have got to choose between the fiddle and the bow. You will want them both.

The Sacraments, duly administered, supply you with the bread of life, the portions of meat in due season ; but the Sacraments will not do you spiritual good unless you have faith to desire and to use them. And, on the other hand, faith looks to the word of Him in whom it believes, and faith can be nothing but a blind faith, or no faith at all, which refuses to feed upon the spiritual nourishment which CHRIST has provided for it. And I hope no one will make this teaching about the necessity of faith an argument against the Apostolic practice of baptizing in their unconscious infancy the children of Christian parents. Who can tell exactly when consciousness in the child

* Rom. v. 2.   † Gal. vi. 15.
‡ *Ibid.*, v. 6.   § 1 Cor. vii. 19.

begins? But the intention of the Church is that the Christian child shall have its life from the very beginning under Christian influences, and shall find the gifts of the new life lodged within its innermost being as soon as ever, under the loving care of its mother, it begins to exercise a half-conscious faith.

There are three remarks that I must add. First, that when I have spoken of faith and Sacrament, as 'necessary to salvation,' I mean necessary *for those who can have them.* Where people have no opportunity of using the Sacraments, GOD can give them strength in His own way. For GOD is not tied to His own instruments. Again, where people have no opportunity of knowing CHRIST, or believing in Him, CHRIST can draw them unknowing, and reveal Himself to them even after death.

Secondly, let me note that faith is a thing of degrees. There is the faith of a converted or converting will—the faith by which a man, perhaps a heathen, first turns to CHRIST to be accepted by Him; and there is the enlightened and stablished faith of a Christian living in the grace of a regenerate life. And in this, too, there are degrees, for we are to go on 'from faith to faith,' till faith be lifted into sight.

Lastly, I have spoken of faith or conversion as practically the same thing. And in fact it is justifiable so to speak of them. Faith is not saving faith except the will go with it; and the conversion of the will towards GOD, suddenly or gradually, is nothing else than the self-committal of true faith, handing over our human life to the government of GOD. You cannot be converted without faith, or really believe without being converted.

THE HOLY EUCHARIST OR HOLY COMMUNION

' Louder than gathered waters,
Or bursting peals of thunder,
    We lift our voice
    And speak our joys,
And shout our loving wonder.

' Angels in fixed amazement
Around our altars hover,
    With eager gaze
    Adore the grace
Of our Eternal Lover :

' Himself and all His fulness,
Who gives to the believer ;
    And by this bread
    Whoe'er are fed
Shall live with GOD for ever !

THE Holy Eucharist is the greatest of the Sacraments, because it stretches so wide and takes in so much, because it is both the Divine feast and the altar of perfect sacrifice and the perfection of brotherly fellowship. And it is also the greatest act of Christian worship, because, with the Lord's Prayer, it is the only act of Christian worship which CHRIST Himself instituted. Matins and evensong, prayer-meeting and Bible-class, are all good ways of approaching GOD in common ; but there is only one form of common worship which sanctifies Sunday and festival according to CHRIST'S intention and the custom of the Church from its very beginnings, and that is the Holy Eucharist, the specially Christian sacrifice, the worship in spirit and in truth.

The Holy Eucharist is so great because CHRIST Himself instituted it, but much more because CHRIST Himself is there present. He is present in the whole of the Christian life. 'Ye are come,' says the Epistle to the Hebrews,* 'unto mount Sion, and unto the heavenly Jerusalem, and to . . . JESUS the mediator of the new covenant.' 'Where two or three are gathered together in My name,' said our LORD Himself, 'there am I in the midst of them.'† But He is specially present, and in a special manner, in the Holy Communion. In that service is every form of devotion : prayer, and confession, and hearing the Word, and profession of faith, and intercession, and adoration, and praise, and oblation—the oblation of the bread and wine, which represent all GOD's gifts to us, given that we may return them to Him in grateful homage—and commemoration, the commemoration of the Passion and resurrection of our LORD. And what a commemoration ! There is commemoration in word and in act by the breaking of the bread and the mingling and outpouring of the cup. This is dramatic. But what a thrilling drama would that be in which the living spirit of Macbeth or Hamlet should crown each representation with his own actual presence ! Yet in the Holy Eucharist all our acts of worship and commemoration are crowned by our LORD's presence, who spiritually, but most really, mingles Himself with our earthly rites and elements, and by the power of the HOLY SPIRIT makes Himself most truly there present amongst us in His body and His blood, under the humble forms of bread and wine.

1. He is there to be our food. Nothing but the very life of GOD can satisfy the need of man. And CHRIST, very GOD made very man, gives Himself in the Holy Communion to be our food. 'He that eateth Me,' He said, 'even he shall live by Me.'‡ How can this be ? It is done through ordinary material channels. By eating bread and drinking

* Heb. xii. 22-24. † St. Matt. xviii. 20.
‡ St. John vi. 57.

wine, the gifts which vegetable gift contributes to our nourishment pass into us, and the gifts of animal life by eating flesh. It is thus, under the expressive veils of the earthly food, bread and wine, which we have duly offered to GOD, that the human and Divine life of the glorified JESUS—His 'flesh,' which is the spiritual essence of His manhood, and the 'blood, which is the life thereof'—is communicated to us. The earthly priest, who represents the whole Christian people, invokes the power of the SPIRIT upon the bread and wine; he blesses them with the recitation of CHRIST'S words of institution, and, lo! in a way which passes our power to fathom, like all the deep things of Nature and grace, the Divine SPIRIT acts upon the earthly elements, and consecrates them, so that invisibly and spiritually, yet really, they become in the midst of the Church the body and blood of the glorified JESUS. Verily, heaven and earth are here mingled and made one.

'Hail, sacred feast, which JESUS makes,
Rich banquet of His flesh and blood!'

2. CHRIST is our food in these holy mysteries, and He is also our sacrifice. Once for all, in the self-sacrifice of His Passion, He offered Himself 'a full, perfect, and sufficient sacrifice, oblation, and satisfaction, for the sins of the whole world.' And He presents Himself for ever in the heavenly place in the power of His once made sacrifice. Here in the Holy Eucharist, then, we are brought near to His heavenly intercession. 'Ye are come . . . unto JESUS the mediator of the new covenant, and unto the blood of sprinkling.'* He, our Priest and Victim, is in the midst of us, unseen, but really with us. And the whole congregation offers or pleads His sacrifice to give effect to all their own imperfect prayers for themselves and others. This is our 'Eucharist'—that is, 'our sacrifice of praise and thanksgiving' in the power of the accepted propitiation.

* Heb. xii. 23.

As Charles Wesley sings:

> ' Thou standest in the holiest place,
> As now for guilty sinners slain;
> Thy blood of sprinkling speaks and prays,
> All-prevalent for helpless man :
>> Thy blood is still the ransom found,
>> And spreads salvation all around.
>
> GOD still respects Thy sacrifice,
> Its savour sweet does always please;
> The offering smokes through earth and skies,
> Diffusing life and joy and peace :
>> To these Thy lower courts it comes,
>> And fills them with Divine perfumes.
>
> ' We need not now go up to heaven
> To bring the long-sought Saviour down.
> Thou art to all that seek Thee given;
> Thou dost e'en now Thy banquet crown :
>> To every faithful soul appear,
>> And show Thy real presence here.'

3. CHRIST our food—CHRIST our sacrifice—CHRIST also the author of our brotherhood. ' Seeing that there is one bread,' says St. Paul, ' we who are many are one body; for we are all partakers of that one bread.'* The Eucharist is a meal of brothers, and their brotherhood is sanctified and deepened by the life of CHRIST there imparted to them and their fellowship in the blessings of His redemption. ' See how these Christians love one another !' cried the heathen in early days. And still—though there are now many more false Christians than there were in the blessed days when unpopularity and persecution kept Christianity pure—still by far the greater part of true human brotherhood in the world comes from the conscious profession of the name of CHRIST and the fellowship in His body and blood. There is a great and growing amount of real Christian love in the world. But, oh, how much more there ought to be ! And we may depend upon it that all large restorations of Christian unity will

* 1 Cor. x. 17.

grow out of those smaller measures of reunion among Christians which arise when those who eat the same bread and drink the same cup are at pains to see that they behave with true brotherly and sisterly love one to another, ' bearing one another's burdens, and so fulfilling the law of CHRIST.'

CHRIST is our food: our sacrifice: our unity. And all these three facts depend one on the other. True it is that communicants may assist at the holy sacrifice of the Eucharist when they are not communicating. Even if we cannot communicate every Sunday, we should strive to be present every Sunday at the holy mysteries. But at the bottom of the matter it will be found that our right to plead the sacrifice depends on our sharing the feast. It is only 'in CHRIST' that we can offer CHRIST—only as members of His body that we can plead in His name. And all that we get from Him we get not for ourselves alone or our own soul's sake merely, but for the whole body. And all our prayers should be for the 'whole estate of CHRIST's Church militant,' for the ingathering of the whole of humanity, and for the perfecting of the whole body of faithful people living and departed. There should be nothing selfish about Eucharistic prayers. Thus, CHRIST our food, CHRIST our sacrifice, CHRIST our unity, is but one CHRIST ; and we cannot have fellowship with Him in one way without having fellowship with Him in all.

'Thanks be to GOD for His unspeakable gift.'

THE APOSTOLIC SUCCESSION

'The Word and Sacraments, the means of grace,
        He duly doth dispense ;
The flourishes of falsehood to deface
        With truth's clear evidence ;
And sin's usurpèd tyranny suppress,
By advancing righteousness and holiness.'

CLEARLY, in Christian churches there must be ministers. How are they to be appointed ? It would seem reasonable that, as they must necessarily be for the advantage or disadvantage of certain bodies of Christian people, these people should have a good deal to say to their appointment. This is reasonable : it is in agreement with our best modern idea of representative and elective government, and also it is in agreement with the ideas of the earliest and best Christian ages. We should never forget that the Christian Church laid great stress on the proper election of Christian ministers by those to whom they were to minister. The first seven deacons were chosen by the 'whole multitude' of Christians before they were ordained by the Apostles. And this precedent was followed for many centuries. In this way the Christian Church gave to the world the first example of representative government.

This idea of the election, or at least the free acceptance, of the clergy by their flocks has remained embedded in the forms of ordination in the Catholic Church, but in most cases it has long since lost all reality. The system of the Middle Ages was against representative government. Tudor and Stuart kings were not more favourable to it.

Thus, the power of making appointments in the Church passed altogether to popes and bishops, kings and patrons.

We need, therefore, in our English Church a great reform. Speaking for the moment only of the appointment of parish priests, we should set ourselves to accomplish at least this—that the nomination of the patron should be communicated to the parishioners before it is confirmed, and that reasonable objections on their part should enable the bishop to require the patron to make another nomination. And, again, when an incumbent had shown himself permanently and seriously incompetent to satisfy the spiritual requirements of his people, a representation by them should enable the bishop to remove him from the cure of souls.

This is not the occasion to discuss details, nor can we enter at all into the questions connected with the appointment of bishops or the reform of the Church's convocations. But this is certain : that such reforms as would give to the laity a real voice in the appointment and removal of their pastors are peremptorily needed.

There is, however, one point which ought to be cleared up before any efforts for practical reform can begin. Who are the laity whose voice ought to be heard with regard to Church appointments ? We mean by these laity Churchmen who are fulfilling their duties as Churchmen, not by any means residents or ratepayers in a certain district. The prophet of Italian democracy, Joseph Mazzini, laid it down that 'political rights are only the correlative of political duties done,' or, in simpler words, 'A man cannot ask to exercise any privilege as a citizen unless he is doing his duties as a citizen.' In the same way, a man cannot exercise any right as a Churchman unless he is doing his duty as a Churchman. A Christian minister ought to have a 'good report of them that are without,'* and Churchmen had better, in the selection of

* 1 Tim. iii. 7.

their ministers, pay a real regard to the public opinion even of those who do not belong to their own body; but they cannot recognise in them any of the formal rights of membership.

So far we have spoken of the true method of electing Church ministers. But the truest possible election does not *make* a man a Church minister; and a bad method of election, though it hinders the efficiency of the minister, does not deprive him, when he is properly ordained, of the spiritual powers which belong to his office. For what is the ministry of the Church? It is a stewardship in the household of GOD. The household, which is the Church, and the stewardship, which is the ministry, are a provision of the Divine bounty to secure that in every place to which the Church reaches, and in each generation, until CHRIST come again, there shall be a due administration of the Divine gifts of truth and grace, and persons qualified to administer them who, by the method of their appointment, shall represent GOD the Giver, and not men the receivers. They are GOD's stewards. So the Apostles called themselves,* and they ordained others to fulfil their office in different grades—deacons,† presbyters,‡ and others, like Timothy and Titus, who held (as far as ministry is concerned) the full Apostolic position. At first it was often the case that these holders of Apostolic position were not any more than the Apostles, locally fixed in a particular church; and while this was so, the name ' bishop' (or local overseer) was given to the presbyters of each church. But after a time there was a slight change in the arrangement of offices, and a corresponding change in the use of the names. Each church came to have an Apostolic officer, who alone came to be called bishop, with presbyters (priests) and deacons under him. Of these the bishop alone has had the general authority

* I Cor. iv. I ; Titus i. 7.
† Acts vi. ; Phil. i. I ; I Tim. iii. 8-13.
‡ Acts xi. 30, xiv. 23, xx. 17-35 ; I Tim. iii. 1-7 ; Titus i. 5-9.

of government, worship and teaching, and in particular the power to ordain others to the sacred ministry, and to lay on hands in Confirmation. The presbyters only have shared with the bishop the right to consecrate the Holy Eucharist and to absolve or readmit penitents; the deacons have held a subordinate office of teaching and ministering. There have been also Minor Orders of subdeacons, readers, door-keepers, acolytes, exorcists, deaconesses, and others, making a rich supply of human ministries in Divine things. Some of these offices have fallen into practical or complete disuse in other parts of the Church and in the English Church. Some of them are now being revived among us. But in regard to the Holy Orders of bishops, priests and deacons, there is no doubt at all that the Church of England has retained them throughout, and now possesses them. We are linked on to the whole of the Catholic Church from the first by this Apostolic succession of ministers, and with the Apostolic succession we have retained the valid administration of all the Sacraments.

What do we mean by *valid?* We mean *ratified, secure.* GOD is not tied to the means of grace of His own institution. Thus, He can give grace freely, and we cannot doubt He has given it where the visible Sacraments are not administered, or not administered duly.

But we are bound to consider the terms of the Divine covenant, the will of our GOD. The ministry is of Divine appointment, and we have no right to tamper with it. Do we not see what havoc has been wrought by men ignoring its value, and so splitting off into a thousand sects? For the Apostolic succession of the ministry was intended to be one of the main pledges for the maintenance of the unity of the body. To maintain unity, and to administer the Divine covenant of grace and truth—this is the purpose of the Christian ministry; and we Churchmen who are determined to recognise and to maintain it had better set ourselves to remove all stumbling-blocks, such as the bad methods of appointment to Church offices, and the lack of means for the removal of incompetent ministers, that the Church may the better fulfil her holy function, being held in good repute by all men.

And we must never forget that there is a false sort of 'sacerdotalism' (that is, belief in these priestly offices) as well as a true. The true kind of 'sacerdotalism' recognises the truth we have just been trying to state. The false 'sacerdotalism' very often does not recognise it; but whether it does or does not, it shows itself by practically transferring to the clergy alone duties and responsibilities which ought to belong to the whole Church. Care for Christian truth, care for religious education and training, care for Christian worship, care for Christian holiness—these things ought not to be left to the clergy. They belong to the whole Church—the whole body of the faithful. And if the clergy wear a solemn dress in the public worship, that is to mark, not the dignity of their own Order, but the dignity of that priestly body which is the whole Church in all its grades, which altogether believes in GOD's Word, and presents itself before Him in holy worship and holy life and holy fellowship of love.

May GOD give to the Church of England now at this time grace to avoid the false 'sacerdotalism,' and to hold the true!

OUR UNSEEN ENEMIES AND FRIENDS

> And is there care in heaven? And is there love
>   In heavenly spirits to these creatures base
> That may compassion of their evils move?
>   There is : else much more wretched were the case
>   Of men than beasts ! but oh ! the exceeding grace
>   Of highest GOD that loves His creatures so,
> And all His works with mercy doth embrace,
>   That blessed angels He sends to and fro
>   To serve to wicked man, to serve his wicked foe.
>
> ' How oft do they their silver bowers leave
>   To come to succour us that succour want !
> How oft do they with golden pinions cleave
>   The flitting skies, like flying pursuivant,
>   Against foul fiends to aid us militant !
> For as they fight they watch and duly ward,
>   And their bright squadrons round about us plant ;
> And all for love, and nothing for reward.
> Oh, why should heavenly GOD to man have such regard?'

WHILE we are speaking of sacramental helps and the supports of Church fellowship, we must not forget the assistance in our spiritual combat which is given us by our unseen personal friends, the saints departed and the angels. Nor, when we are thinking of them, can we forget our unseen personal enemies, the malignant spirits who have fallen into enmity with GOD—Satan and his angels. The belief in angels and devils our LORD found among the Jews when He came. It is, indeed, an instinctive belief in one shape or another all over the world. But our LORD by constant and emphatic statements both purged the belief of the perils of superstition, and confirmed it to us as part of our Christian heritage. No one who believes

in Him as the absolutely trustworthy teacher can doubt
that we really do have dealings with good and bad spirits
—angels and devils.

1. We all know how we are tempted by our own flesh
and by the world of men around us. But there are
temptations which seem to come, and which our Lord
teaches us do come, from another source. Sometimes
there is shot into our mind a thought so poisonous, so
foul, yet so distinct and vivid, that it seems like nothing
but the suggestion of an unseen bad companion. So it
very likely is, and we must remember that the mere
suggestion is no more our fault than if it came from a
human companion. Sometimes there surges in our mind
so evil a tempest of pride and rebellion against God's
sovereignty that it seems to come from the very leader of
all that in the universe is in rebellion against God. So it
probably does, and we can be on our guard against it
accordingly. Sometimes we are utterly in despair, and a
voice tells us that it is no use trying—that all men are
really bad at bottom, and we cannot do better than follow
our nature; the seemingly good men are not much better
than hypocrites when we come to know them, or, if there
are good men, they are made of different material from us;
certainly *we* cannot be anything else than bad, so it is no
use trying. That voice comes from 'the devil,' that means
'the slanderer'* of men, the king of all cynics, the only
inspirer of thoughts of despair. Or once more, do we not
often feel that we are deceived in regard to sin—that
because we were not watchful a sinful course of action
presents itself to us in quite false colours, and we are led
to follow it till it is too late to draw back, and then it
seems as if everything conspired to show us how deluded
we have been? This is the 'deceitfulness of sin,' the chief
device of the 'father of lies,' who makes all the false
prophets and deceivers of men his mouthpieces and agents.†

* Job i. 9-12 ; Zech. iii. 1, 2 ; Rev. xii. 10.
† Heb. iii. 13 ; 2 Thess. ii. 10 ; Isa. xxx. 10 ; John viii. 44.

Yes, Satan, 'the adversary,' 'the prince of the power of the air,'* and all his hosts of darkness, are real beings, who really tempt us as they tempted our LORD. They are at the root of all the moral and much of the physical evil of the world. But as Satan was utterly overcome by our LORD, so that he fled away from His victorious manhood to hide his head in hell, so we, who have the very spirit of JESUS within us, can fight in His Name and strength, and share His victory. And the victories which in the Name of JESUS we win in the hour of temptation are only the foretaste of the day when Satan and all his angels shall be manifestly put under the feet of the victorious Son of Man.

2. Meanwhile, as we have devils to tempt us, we have also angels to guard and help us. We know very little about the angels, but we are told that they worship GOD and behold His face, and that they are ministering spirits for the Divine purposes both of mercy and of judgment.† Sometimes, indeed, their presence has been made perceptible as men to men—as to Mary, the mother of our LORD, at the moment of the Annunciation, and to the holy women after the resurrection, and to Peter in the prison. But our LORD speaks of them as pure spirits without sensual natures. He leads us also to think of them as attached as guardians to little children; and the Apostles believed them to assist at the worship of the Church on earth, and to attend the members of the Church in their perils, and to learn from the Church fresh depths of the wisdom and love of GOD.‡ And when we think how full the universe is of beauties and traits of Divine wisdom, of which men are never witnesses, it is a comfort to remember that we are not the only intelligent creatures of GOD, and that it may well be that angels, of whom we know so little, find their joy and their occasion for wor-

* Eph. ii. 2.   † Heb. i. 14; St. Matt. xxv. 31, xxvi. 53.
‡ St. Matt. xviii. 10, xxii. 30; Acts xii. 15; 1 Cor. xi. 10; Eph. iii. 10.

shipping GOD in all the evidences of beauty and wisdom
which the great universe supplies. So our human ministries
and our human worship seem but little parts of a great
universal ministry of Divine service and praise, of which
the angels are the instruments, or, as it were, the medi-
tating priests. It may be, for all we know, that there is
no creature of GOD which has not a corresponding spirit
of intelligence, high or low—a representative angel.

3. But besides the angels we have other unseen personal
helpers—the blessed and holy dead. They have ceased
to live in our world, but they are alive to GOD, and in the
' Communion of the Saints ' we have fellowship with them.
' Ye are come,' says the Apostolic writer to the Hebrew
Christians, ' unto mount Zion, and unto the city of the
living GOD, to the heavenly Jerusalem, and to the innumer-
able hosts of angels . . . and to the spirits of just men
made perfect.'*   Not only with angels, then, are we
brought into fellowship, but with the blessed departed.
How much they know about us we cannot tell. Nothing
is revealed to us. Whether we can have personal intercourse with them by asking their prayers personally for us
in our need we cannot tell for certain. It may well be
that it is in order that we may worship GOD only—the
FATHER, and our Divine and human LORD, and the HOLY
SPIRIT—that this knowledge is withheld from us. But we
do *know* that they in the unseen world are waiting, like us,
for the coming of the kingdom of our LORD in glory,
and that we can join our prayer with theirs before the
heavenly altar, that there may be no more delay ; and we
think that they are witnesses of how we acquit ourselves
in the struggle which they fought so bravely, and handed
on to us to finish. Probably we do not gain half the
strength we might from this thought of the Communion
of Saints. The blessed dead are not separated from the
Church ; they are only the most advanced part of the
Church. They are not only our examples in holy living,

* Heb. xii. 22-24.

nor is it only that we owe to them the heritage of our holy faith: it is also the fact that we and they live one life of prayer and praise and faith in one body in CHRIST. With them we believe, and hope, and love, and pray— with Mary, the pure and glorious Virgin Mother: with the woman who was a sinner, but who, 'greatly forgiven,' has 'greatly loved': with patriarchs and prophets and apostles: with martyrs and confessors—men, women, and children: with holy teachers and wise pastors and matrons: with those who were conspicuous in holiness, and are held in universal memory as saints: and with those, too, whose struggles and whose victories were known to few or to none, but who 'lived faithfully hidden lives and rest in unvisited graves.' With all these we are one, and to see and know all these will one day be part of the glory of the vision of GOD.

And meanwhile, while we cannot see them, still they are by far the largest part of the Catholic Church. And it is a comfort, when we are deploring the divisions of the Church, to reflect that it is only, as it were, the lower limbs of the body of CHRIST that are on earth. However divided here, all true-hearted followers of CHRIST are held in fellowship by their common union with our LORD, and also by their union with the Church in paradise, whither the divisions which human sin has caused cannot penetrate. There are no sects or divisions among faithful Christians after death. 'And as,' says St. Augustine, 'the whole CHRIST is made up of the head and the body, the head is our Saviour himself, and the body is His Church: not this Church or that, but the Church scattered over the whole world; not the Church which at present exists on earth, but the Church to which those also belong who were before us, and who shall be after us to the end of the world.'

THE OTHER SIDE OF DEATH

'Therefore to whom turn I but to Thee, the ineffable Name
    Builder and Maker, Thou, of houses not made with hands!
What, have fear of change from Thee who art ever the same?
    Doubt that Thy power can fill the heart that Thy power
        expands?
There can never be one lost good! What was shall live as·
        before ;
    The evil is null, is nought, is silence implying sound :
What was good shall be good, with, for evil, so much good
        more ;
    On the earth, the broken arcs ; in the heaven, a perfect
        round.'

NOTHING is more certain than that we all shall die.*
Nothing is more certain to one who believes in JESUS
CHRIST than that death will be for no one of us the end
of life. Thus, if death has a terror for us, it is not so
much because of what it can destroy as because of what
it cannot : because it neither destroys nor changes our
souls, our true selves. We are so apt to speak of dead
people as if they were quite different from what in truth
they were, that we get to think of death as if it changed
our character; but it does not : it only transplants us out
of this world, with which we are so familiar, into another
world—transplants us, with the character which in this
world we have made for ourselves unchanged, into that
unfamiliar world beyond, where GOD is waiting to see us
judge ourselves as He judges us. There, on the other side
of death, there is no public opinion to give us a sense of

* For my present purpose, I mean the word to cover any 'change'
which brings our mortal life to an end (1 Cor. xv. 50-52).

91

security in wrong-doing or neglecting GOD'S law, no wife or husband or friends to assure us ' it must be all right, for so many people do so,' no dissipations or occupations to distract us from the thought of GOD ; but only solitude and an awful silence, in which we shall see ourselves, perhaps for the first time, as we are, irretrievably, in the tremendous light of GOD. There is a great deal about the unseen world beyond the grave that we do not know at all, or do not certainly know. But here I will give the first place to that we seem certainly to know on the authority of our LORD or by the witness of our own consciences.

1. *We know for certain, as I have said, that death is not the end of life.* The human soul or spirit is at death separated from the dead body. The body rests in the sleep of death. The human spirit is said by our LORD to ' live to GOD.' What the life of our spirit without our body can be we cannot imagine. All that we know by experience is life *in* a body, and that is our natural state and will be our eternal state, for—

2. *We believe for certain in the Resurrection of the Body.* This does not mean that the particles of our former bodies, which were laid in the grave and which have decayed and passed into all sorts and forms of natural life, will be collected together again; but it means that we in our same selves shall be reclothed in a spiritual body, which we shall recognise as our own body, probably because it will, as it were, take the form and impress of our own unchanged selves. Any way, GOD will give to each a body as it shall please Him—a spiritual body.* In this life the men of science assure us that every thought we think with our minds has corresponding to it a change in the material substance of our brains. But this correspondence of soul and body will be, we suppose, much more perfect in a spiritual body. The substance of the spiritual body will surely be as much more fine and

* 1 Cor. xv.

delicate than our present body as the ether is more fine
and delicate than common matter. Thus, our spiritual
body will be simply the expression of ourselves. Here,
we know, our body half conceals our true selves. There,
all we are or think or feel will express itself (we must
suppose) without effort or trouble or possibility of con-
cealment or misunderstanding in our glorious, painless,
resurrection bodies. At any rate, resurrection bodies we
shall have—for good, and must I not say for evil also?
For if our spiritual bodies then express and do not con-
ceal our true selves, our very bodies may be our condemnation in that day of resurrection which is the
resurrection of life to some, the resurrection of judgment
to others.*

3. *For with our Resurrection is certainly connected our Last
Judgment;* and this judgment is not only a judgment on
our single selves, but also a general judgment on all mankind and on the whole universe of beings. The Day of
Judgment! Who can picture it? The day when all
lies and frauds are exposed, and nothing can resist the
truth; when all wrongs are made right, and all oppressions
and injustices and cruelties are utterly overthrown, under
the burning wrath of CHRIST; and when the meek, the
friends of CHRIST, triumphantly, and before the eyes of all
men, possess the earth: the day when every thing and
person will seem utterly and simply what it is in CHRIST'S
sight, whose truth and meekness and righteousness shall
be everywhere and manifestly supreme: the day when all
riddles shall be solved, and all the mystery of pain and
sorrow interpreted in the glory and triumph of the Lamb
that was slain. We cannot picture the day to ourselves,
but we can believe in it and let the absolute certainty of
its coming expel out of our soul everything that cannot
bear the eternal light.

4. *And after the Day of Judgment is Heaven*—the perfect
life where men, being at last perfectly what men ought to .

* St. John v. 29.

be in soul and body, live the perfect life in the perfect
city; adoring GOD, the THREE in ONE, with all the
angelic hosts : beholding GOD in all things, and all things
in GOD : enjoying all the richness of universal truth and
beauty, all the joy of mutual love and fellowship and
service, in a progress which can never end, where there
can never be lack of novelty or variety, so infinite is the
richness of the being of GOD in whom all spirits live.

5. *And after the Day of Judgment there is also Hell*, the
place or state of the punishment of the wicked—that
punishment which is sometimes described in the New
Testament as if it were the result of a sentence pro-
nounced by the Divine Judge, like a punishment in a
court of law ;* sometimes as if it were the natural consequence of sin, like failure, or disease in this life.† This
punishment of the lost is pictured in our minds under
figures of outer darkness and fire and worms, figures
which suggest to our mind a state of outcast misery and
pain and remorse.

About this punishment of hell there has been a great
deal of unwarranted teaching that has done a vast
amount of harm, because it has seemed quite inconsistent
with our sense of the Divine justice or love. Thus, it is a
monstrous crime to teach that any are created by GOD
such that they cannot escape the punishment of hell, or
that any can be 'lost' simply because they did not know
the truth of the Gospel, like the heathen ; or because, like
many in Christian countries, they had no real opportunity
of knowing and serving GOD. We can be quite certain
that GOD 'willeth all men to be saved,' and that, if not
in this life, then beyond it, He will give the fullest chances
of knowing and loving Him to each soul whom He has
created. Again, it is quite without warrant that any have
presumed to say that the majority of mankind, or any
particular proportion of mankind, will be finally lost.
About this and about a multitude of other matters we

* St. Matt. xxv. 41.   † 2 Cor. v. 10.

know nothing. But when all these mistakes in teaching have been recognised and corrected, there still remains the terrible truth of which we are assured from the lips of the Incarnate Love, JESUS CHRIST, our LORD, that it is possible for men to hate the Divine light because it interferes with their own lusts or pride; possible for them to go on hating it till they harden themselves against it, till good becomes evil to them, and evil good, till their state is like that of Satan, and they sin an ' eternal sin ' which ' shall not be forgiven either in this world or in the world to come '*—a sin which shall not be forgiven, surely, only because those who sin it have rendered themselves at last incapable of repenting or desiring to love GOD.

It is, I think, quite impossible to read the words of our LORD about wilful sin, and to suppose that He would allow us to think or to teach that everything must come right at the last for every soul. We had better confess that there is very much we do not know, but that there are those of whom we shall say at the last, ' Good were it for them if they had never been born.'†

5. *As to the middle state of waiting between death and judgment we know almost nothing.* The best of us die imperfect, and some, whose final salvation we yet confidently expect, very imperfect and ignorant. Therefore we cannot but think that, in the waiting state, men are cleansed and enlightened ; and this enlightening and cleansing can hardly be without pain. So we cannot but suppose. And so Christians have prayed for the departed that they may find peace, and mercy, and refreshment, and light, in that dim abode of mingled joy and pain. It is not without a Divine purpose that nothing is certainly told us about this middle state. Only we thankfully learn from the words of St. Peter about those who perished in the Flood, that the ' Gospel ' can be ' preached to them

* St. Matt. xii. 32 ; St. Mark iii. 29.
† St. Matt. xxvi. 24.

that are dead also,' so that even death may become to men the occasion and opportunity of a new life.*

We have touched on what we know little about. What we do know certainly is enough for us to live by. We know that our daily acts form habits, and habits become character, and character tends to become fixed and unchangeable for evil or good. We know that beyond death is judgment, and that the final judgment is to be the restoration of all things to the place for which they were created, or for which they have fitted themselves, in the universe of GOD, which is the kingdom of CHRIST. Everywhere shall be a Divine order. Every will and heart shall acknowledge this order, and shall adore the sovereignty, the justice, the goodness of GOD. 'At the name of JESUS every knee shall bow, of things in heaven, and things in earth, and things under the earth; and every tongue shall confess that JESUS CHRIST is LORD, to the glory of GOD the FATHER.'†

* St. Pet. iv. 6   † Phil. ii. 10, 11.

9 781610 974431